Nicolette Baumeister

New Landscape Architecture

BRAUN

Imprint

The Deutsche Bibliothek is registering this publication in the Deutsche Nationalbibliographie; detailed bibliographical information can be found on the Internet at http://dnb.ddb.de

ISBN 978-3-938780-25-1

© 2007 by Verlagshaus Braun
www.verlagshaus-braun.de

1st edition 2007

Selection of projects: Nicolette Baumeister
Project coordination: Stephan Goetz
Editorial staff: Nicolette Baumeister, Hanna Pitz
Final Editing: Anna Hinc, Franziska Nauck
Translation: allround Fremdsprachen GmbH Cord von der Lühe, Stephen Roche
Graphic design and Layout: Michaela Prinz
Reproduction: LVD Gesellschaft für Datenverarbeitung mbH, Berlin
Litho: tiff.any GmbH, Berlin

Contents

Contents

New Landscape Architecture

Geometrically designed gravel borders, austere lighting stelae, stratified railway tracks, colourful sculptured islands, mighty concrete cubes. Open spaces that go beyond traditional garden design put our conventional way of seeing things to a hard test, and force us to question the familiar. The design elements within new landscape architecture have come a long way from their traditional models. Public space is now manifested either in more or less impressive forms. Trends and events also play an ever greater role in landscape architecture, where easily consumable images are often more readily accepted than the idea of sustainable living spaces. So are we losing sight of the role landscape architecture plays in supporting and promoting new social and cultural movements? Not a whit!

Landscape architecture today is rising to meet new challenges, and fulfilling a new role. Today landscape architecture is rarely concerned with traditional tasks such as the classical design of gardens or parks. Today's challenges lie in redefining urban wastelands, regenerating deindustrialised land, giving new life to former industrial spaces and protecting the ecology of disused opencast mines. Undertakings such as these call for an approach that goes beyond traditional artistic or creative roles. They call for the courage to question received values and a readiness to experiment with new ideas, coupled with a large measure of expertise and an expressive energy that is sensitive to the aesthetics of its environment.

Examples such as the Welzow-Süd opencast mining area in eastern Germany demonstrate how architectural landscaping interventions that are part of a long-term plan can influence and direct larger processes of change.

That is not to say that the few remaining relics of opencast mining are merely to be regarded as novel design elements. Rather, they are part of a general plan to translate, on a grand scale, the remnants of the industrial mining process into a new topographical aesthetic.

above:
Desert/Oasis Welzow
planning: bgmr Landscape
Architects and
archiscape

below:
Post-Industrial Park,
Eberswalde State Horticultural
Show 2002
planning: TOPOTEK 1

Preface

Often it is temporary projects, such as national or regional garden shows, that make it possible to realise innovative ideas. Moreover, exhibitions such as these that attract widespread publicity make an important contribution to a debate in which not only experts but also, more particularly, the general public must participate. They prompt discussion and debate about our urban environments, thereby encouraging new developments, as was the case with the State Horticultural Show in Eberswalde in 2002. In this instance the redevelopment of a former industrial zone focused less on staging an encounter with industrial romanticism and more on mapping the terrain so as to provide visitors with a sense of orientation. Similarly, the National Horticultural Show that was held in Munich in 2005, with its highbrow and austere contributions to the theme of nature, offered a carefully considered representation of ecological conditions and aesthetic effects in the field of landscape architecture and public space. Although this large-scale event failed to arouse enthusiasm among large sections of the population, by addressing their senses it certainly gave many people cause to reflect.

Appealing to the senses and provoking reflection is exactly what the projects documented in this book should do. The selection contained here covers both private and public projects. In addition to looking at larger and better known projects we also focused on smaller projects that have flourished in obscurity; projects such as the Cabinet Garden in the Munich Residenz or the Municipal Gardens in Weingarten.

The projects featured in this book provide a composite and representative portrait of the spectrum of contemporary landscape architecture in the German-speaking regions and show just how varied is the role played by landscape architecture today. Certain elements that may appear unintelligible at first glance are in fact precociously forward-looking. Sometimes distinctly and strikingly, at other times unobtrusively and naturally. But always aesthetically, and with energy and individuality.

Nicolette Baumeister

above:
Redesigning the
Kabinettsgarten,
Residenz Munich
planning: Peter Kluska

below:
BUGA München 2005
(Munich National
Horticultural
Show 2005)
planning: Rainer Schmidt
Landscape Architects

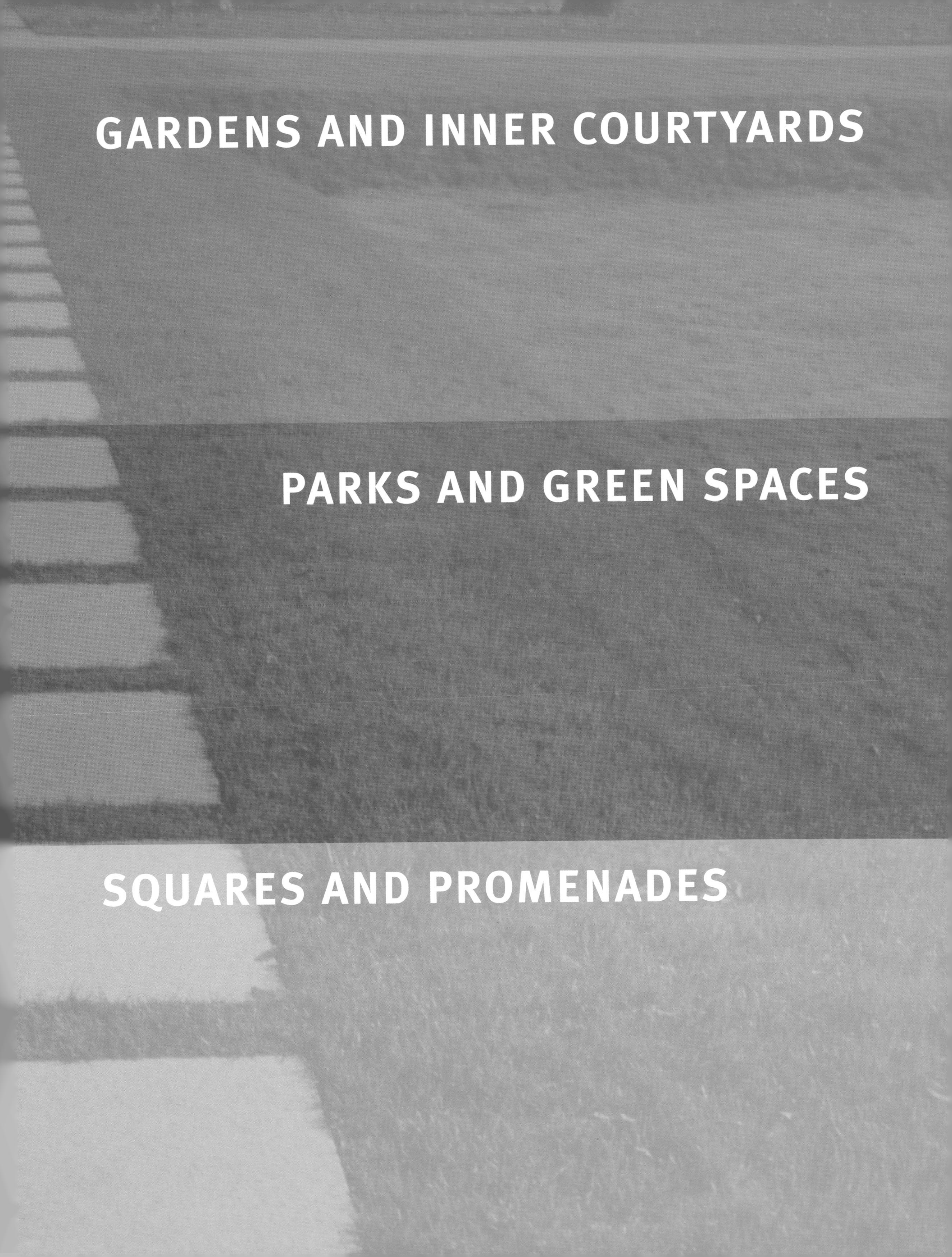

GARDENS AND INNER COURTYARDS

PARKS AND GREEN SPACES

SQUARES AND PROMENADES

keller landscape architects

Inner Courtyard Restoration Lothringer Strasse

Franz Damm (*1974) has been a partner
since 2005 in this practice, founded by
Regine Keller (*1962). For both of them,
landscape-architectural planning means
coming to terms with different forms of
nature in the context of a city or the open
countryside and constantly reformulating
them – as part of urban culture, or as a
new interpretation of landscape. Their
aim is not a trend, but an individual idea
for a specific location.

Munich

As part of works to close a gap between buildings caused by suburban-railway construction, an underground garage was built to the south-east of the courtyard, which meant it was necessary to redesign the inner courtyard. The planners succeeded in persuading the owners of the adjoining properties – of whom there were more than twenty – to join a collaborative project. Carried out in association with Ziller+ Architects and Town Planners, this project now unites six courtyard subsections, previously separated by walls and fences, to form one communal courtyard. A major element in this planning process was the participation by the tenants and by the staff of the children's and young people's center in the courtyard. I Broad private forecourts were constructed along the facades on the courtyard side, intended as secure areas for individual use. Towards the middle the space is devoted to the children's and young people's center, inviting the visitor to sit on the grass, or to play on the various play facilities. Diagonal paths between the buildings and the underground garage give access to the courtyard of an optimum kind. The crossings on the paths, forming a link between the individual buildings and the entrance to the underground car park, are of small-stone granite, laid as irregular paving. The lawns are divided from the paths by unwrought steel strips, laid up to 20 cm high at points where the levels of the underground car park make this necessary. I The surrounding paving was removed from the places where the old trees stand; these surroundings are now of gravel and are water-permeable. Two new groves of trees, a grove of mountain ash and one of wild cherries, form a light ceiling of leaves, generously supplementing the older trees which remain.

above:
Raised levels make it possible
to plant trees over the roof of
the underground garage
below:
Paved paths link the entrances
to the communal courtyard

Project Facts
Builder-owner: Münchner Gesellschaft für
Stadterneuerung mbH (MGS)
Building Time: 2002–2004
Size: 2,400 m²
Further Participants:
Marie-Therese Okresek Architects,
underground garage:
Ziller + Architects and Town Planners

above left:
The ventilation ports of the underground garage also serve as seats along the play area. Daylight enters the underground garage through glass elements and the artificial lighting in the parking spaces shines out into the courtyard
below left:
Paths directly linking the entrances are the main feature of the inner courtyard
right:
Playground and sports area

ver.de landscape architecture with Brigitte Golling

Inner Courtyard Restoration Wiener Platz

The company was founded in the year 2000 by Birgit Kröniger, Jochen Rümpelein and Robert Wenk. The team plans and builds public and private open spaces in an urban and rural context. It has set itself the goal of developing an individual, contemporary solution of the highest quality in design, ecology and function for each planning task, exploiting the potential of the site in question.

Munich   The interior courtyard at Wiener Platz 7 in Munich is surrounded by five-story buildings built at the end of the 19th century. Prior to restoration, large parts of the courtyard were taken up by a back building used as a workshop. The residual area, asphalted and treeless, served as a delivery zone and storage area. I A part of the back building, with flats, loading areas and studios, was restored in the course of engineering works, and the former workshop was replaced by a compact, two-storey loft building. By reducing the built-over area, it was possible at the same time to create an interior courtyard for common use by the building's occupants and employees, featuring a wide range of development and recreational functions such as rainwater infiltration or green roofs. The redesign also reflected a wide range of ecological considerations. The courtyard, formerly sealed off, was planted with trees, shrubs, bushes and turf suitable for the site, while climbing plants were used to green the walls and facades. I The courtyard is divided into clearly defined subsections. The approach to the loft building is via large slabs of Rinchnach granite in rows, running from the thoroughfare on the Wiener Platz through a gravel surface shaded by snowy mespilus. A fountain of black granite overlays the noise of the surrounding streets with its splashing sound. A grassy area with a sand pit and sculptural play facilities serves as a meeting place for the inhabitants of different ages. In front of the walls, on the parapets and in the light-shafts on the loft building, beds have been planted with sun-absorbing or shade-compatible shrubs. The three serviceberry trees in the center of the courtyard reflect the seasons.

above left:
The courtyard is a meeting place for the residents and a new "address" for the businesses there
above right:
Autumnal serviceberries in front of the loft building
below:
Seats beneath dwarf serviceberries

Project Facts
Builder-owner: Franz, Georg and Xaver Engelhard, Munich
Building Time: 2001
Size: 600 m²

above left:
Stepped beds with lavender, sage, globe thistles and purple coneflowers
above right:
The courtyard in an exciting dialogue of living and working in an urban context

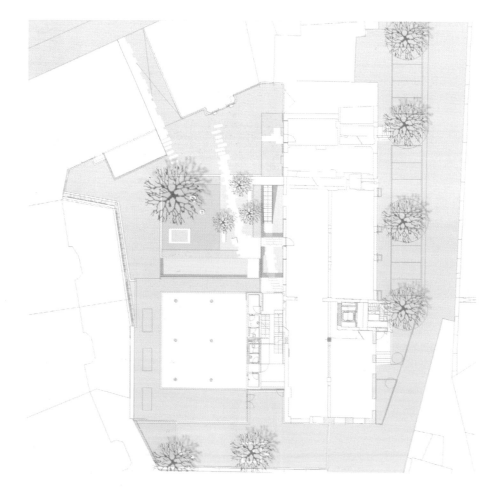

below left:
Site plan
below right:
"Peep" from the passage to the Wiener Platz; Fountain on the paved path

atelier loidl-reisch

Cordula Loidl-Reisch works in a wide range of fields, including roof and facade greening as well as garden-monument maintenance. Behind all her designs stand the following principles: the human being at the center – work at the interface of innovation, patina and atmosphere – tailor-made solutions for open spaces and their users – urban "limitation" as a design challenge – resource-oriented planning.

Benedictine Monastery Admont, Inner Courtyard

Admont

Following major revitalisation work and modifications to an art museum in the Benedictine seminary at Admont improvements are now scheduled to be made to the seminary's inner courtyard. With missing historical structures precluding faithful reconstruction the architect's task was to arrive at a fresh interpretation of the premises while respecting the listed status of the building. Sections of the monastery had lain in ruins since a fire in the mid-19th century and had been only partially rebuilt: the two small former courtyards had been amalgamated into a rectangular yard 157 metres long and 69 metres wide. | A clear, orthogonal style was chosen for the exterior space, in contrast to the baroque architecture of the monastery, resulting in a modern garden area set in a historical environment. Although the inner courtyard of the seminary displayed a certain arbitrariness in its original design the existing elements were to be accorded the respect that their different values demanded. The old concentric rings of roses around the baroque Neptune fountain, for example, were incorporated into the new design but now had the shape of perfectly circular flowerbeds. | The ground surface immediately adjacent to the buildings was rendered in fine cobbling to improve the visual definition of the monastery complex as a whole. Beyond this cobbling an area of grass, vegetation and paths extends outwards, its relief and raised steel verges conferring an impression of plasticity on the surrounding land. | A sunken lawn marks the location of the original buildings destroyed in the fire. Two narrow, raised pathways cross this sunken lawn, their granite stepping stones embedded in the turf. The space is marked by a meandering hedge. A 400-year old design has given rise to a maze symbolising every person's journey to his or her inner core.

above:
View from the barred window of the world's biggest baroque monastery library onto the inner monastery courtyard
below:
Sunken-garden relief with embankment road on the site of the former building complex

Project Facts
Builder-owner:
Benedictine Monastery Admont
Building Time: 2000
Size: 1.1 ha

above:
Allium christophii in
a circle of roses
below:
Lush carpets of flowers frame
the labyrinth on both sides
right:
Plan for the inner monastery
courtyard

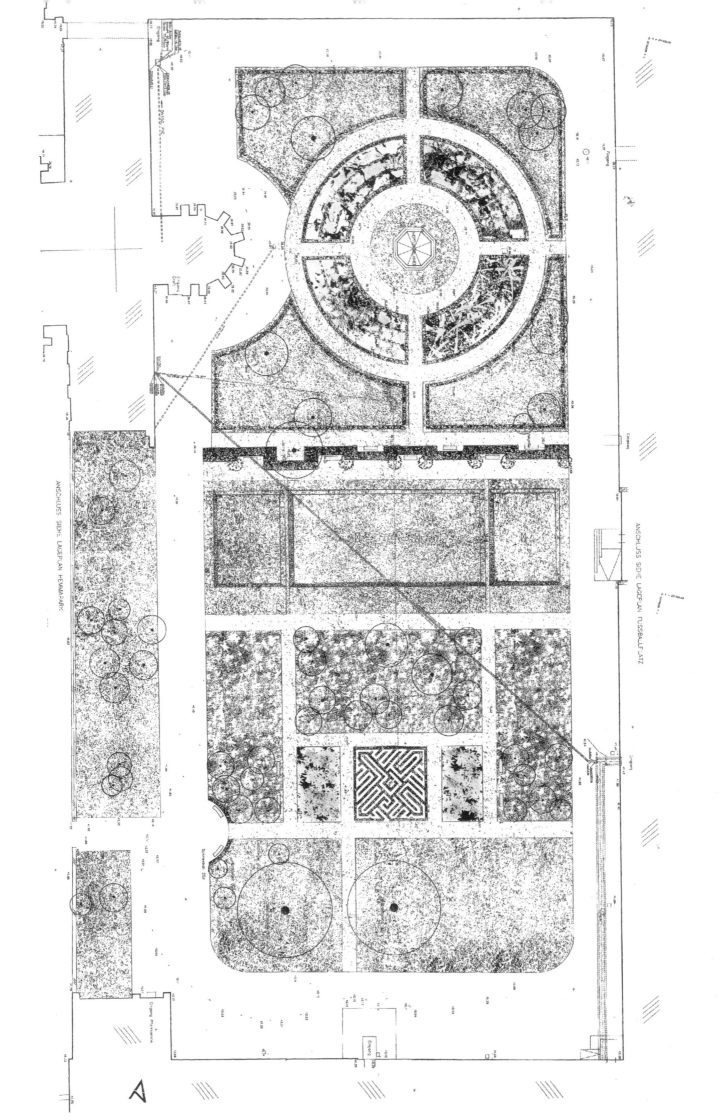

bauchplan).(baldauf . otto . okresek

Inner Courtyard Renngasse

Vienna   A prominent building in the center of Vienna has been rebuilt and renovated to create a prime office complex. The view from the windows of the offices overlooking the courtyard offers many interesting sights despite the reduction to a few strong visual elements: white marble silicic forms the horizontal spaces, strewn glass pellets (round, polished glass shards) glisten like mirrors on a surface of water. Round and floating, anthracite-coloured concrete plates float like water lily blossom on the gravel. I An image of a peaceful, introverted courtyard is created which reveals a constantly changing picture as a result of the different light effects and reflections. From every angle of the courtyard, which is enclosed by a bridge construction, new unique yard shapes are revealed. The Schottenpark to the north forms a green background. The reflection in the facades is continued forever by the abstract, poetic garden image. I Flexible elements create dynamism: water plates generate sound characteristics and improve the micro-climate – the meditative atmosphere contrasts the workday routine inside the building. Individual concrete cylinders penetrate the gravel space as seating elements. Along the edges and in areas to gather there are more of them. In the courtyard itself, the green is stylised through bamboo plants. In powder-covered plant containers, the bamboo as a refined vertical element draws looks from the courtyard level up to the upper floors. From the inlaid atrium a clematis envelops the yard vertically towards the bridge construction. The courtyard attempts to avert the attention from what is actually there (a light gravel, round concrete plates, a few bamboo plants) to what could be there: the view of an urban landscape which continues forever beyond the frame of a picture.

Graduate landscape architects Tobias Baldauf, Florian Otto and Marie-Theres Okresek direct their interests to the ordinary, to what is in process, and to a search for the potential concealed here for public and private open spaces. Identifying this potential and transforming it into experienced space of a specific kind, and into improved qualities of life – this is what they expect from bauchplan).(, a freelance network.

above:
The courtyard continues infinitely through the reflection in the facades
below:
Floating concrete plates in the glistening courtyard

Project Facts
Builder-owner: Amisola Immobilien AG and Deloitte Austria (tenant)
Building Time: 2004
Size: 357 m²
Architects: A.C.C Ziviltechniker Gmbh / Peter Klein
Further Participants: Dorothée Hock, Reinhard Micheller
Art Consultation: Yuji Oshima

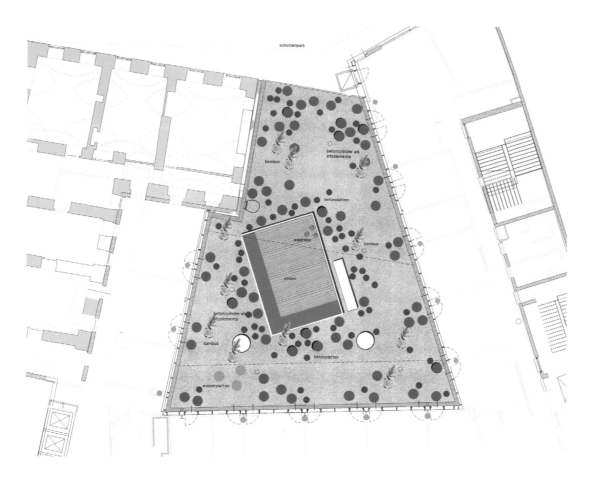

above left:
The introverted courtyard with
the carved Atrium benefits
from the adjoining
Schottenpark as green background

below left and right:
The users of the neighbouring
office buildings are invited by
concrete cylinders functioning
as seating elements

Landscape Architecture and Urban Development Bode ▪ Williams + Partners

St. Jakobi Church Square

Rostock

The Late Gothic church of St. Jakobi was hit in an air raid in 1942 and completely destroyed in the post-war years. The new design was planned to give some of its original dignity back to the square, while developing it into a modern urban area. Putting this complex design into practice – incorporating the results of archaeological excavations – presented a particular challenge. **I** Across the square in a diagonal runs a deliberately designed, curved fold in the ground, representing a stylised boundary between old and new. The southern half shows the archaeological excavations. Here, in the "factual recollection" area, work has revealed layers of history. Remains of the old church foundations and crypts have been incorporated into the design, and steel edging shows the ground plan of the gothic church. **I** The northern half of the square represents the section of "rational recollection" – at this point you are both above the church and in it. The lawn is divided by bronze lines and plaques, testifying to those parts of the church which were particularly valuable in an architectural and art-historical context: the altar, the pulpit, the throne and font. The sparing use of plants and artefacts means that the square remains spacious and light. **I** The northern boundary and edge is formed by the colonnade, a tall and filigree construction, reminding the onlooker of the spiritual space of the gothic church. The way it is planted also contains a reference to the history of this spot: in its reduced form and colour, this is intended to underline the whole intention of the design – the pale green shadows of the shrubs and grass represent the transience of earthly life. As a contrast, twelve tall, pyramid-shaped holly trees symbolise the immortality of the spirit. An old apple tree has been replanted, as a symbol of paradise.

Udo Bode and Peter Braun look on landscape architecture as a symbiosis of landscape design and architecture. They are particularly interested in the development of landscape-architectural solutions of a sustainable, high-quality kind. It is important to seek and crystallise the characteristics which are quintessential to the project, to be derived from the genius of the location in question, as well as a holistic approach.

above:
Upper level with view of colonnade
below:
View of the upper and lower level

Project Facts
Builder-owner: Rostocker Gesellschaft für Stadtentwicklung (RGS)
Building Time: 2002–2004
Size: 1 ha
Conception: Henschel + Webersinke with Niclas Dünnebacke

above left:
View eastwards, "factual
recollection" area
above right:
View southwards from the
colonnade
below:
Sectional view and detail

Schnittansicht Beläge und Einfassungen

Aufsicht Einfriedungsmauer Pädagogien-Str

Abwicklung Einfriedungsmauer Pädagogien-Str

ANSICHT PADAGOGIENSTRASSE

Ansicht Torelement Apostelstraße

Ansicht Torelement Pädagogien-Str

Ansicht Torelement Bei der Jakobikirche

Detail Verlegemuster

Ansicht Lehnenbank Typ Chorgestuhl

Schnittansicht Kollonade

Ansicht Kollonade An der Jakobikirche

above left:
View eastwards
above right:
Boundary fold in the ground
and remains of foundations
bordered by Corten steel
below:
Site plan

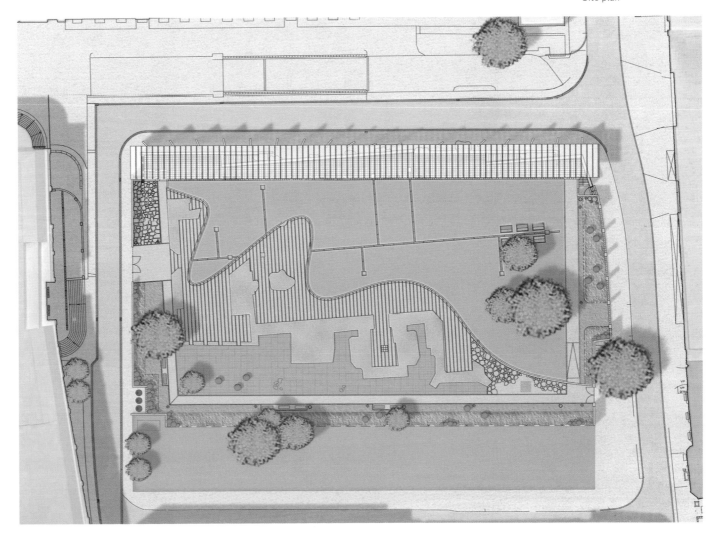

WES & Partners

The practice WES & Partners Landscape Architects has been in existence for 36 years and is managed by Hinnerk Wehberg, Peter Schatz, Wolfgang Betz and Michael Kaschke. The tasks of the practice cover the development of interior and building architecture: open space and project planning, the planning of green spaces and landscapes, certificates and urban planning projects as well as building art.

Redesigning the Jungfernstieg

Hamburg

An international competition announced in 2002 offered entrants the challenge of developing the Jungfernstieg once again into a grand overall space with multiple uses. The area between the Inner Alster, the Little Alster and the square Rathausmarkt was regaining its function as a sort of stage, a place of meeting and performance. Because of street building works and other constructional activities, the water had been pushed ever further from the line of buildings at this spot – the point of contact between city and water threatened to fall apart. I The plan produced by the landscape architects, developed in collaboration with the architect André Poitiers, envisages removing these disrupting barriers, to create space again for as diverse a range of uses as possible and to re-create its relation to the Alster. Planning involves threefold division of the complex between the Inner Alster, the Little Alster and the Rathausmarkt. The street area will be narrowed and given an enlarged pedestrian zone in front of the facades. A boulevard is being built on the water side, with a bisected triaxial avenue of lime trees. This will be adjoined by a spacious flight of steps, like a grandstand, covering the whole width of the Jungfernstieg and leading to the water. On these steps individual benches can be placed together to form endless rows, providing a flexible grandstand for various different events, which can be held right on the water. I There will be no large or complex emplacements, to create natural and uncluttered surroundings – only a new square pavilion will stand partly on the new steps, replacing a building from the seventies.

above:
Jungfernstieg in October 2005
below:
Completed central section

Project Facts
Builder-owner: Free and Hanseatic City of Hamburg
with the Association Lebendiger Jungfernstieg e.V.
Building Time: 2003–2006
Size: 37,500 m²

above left:
Movable bench
above right:
Visualisation of
Jungfernstieg by day

below left:
View from front and
ground plan
below right:
Visualisation of lighting
design

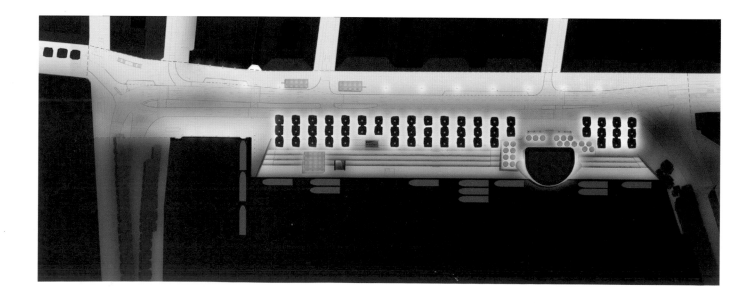

Bendfeldt · Schröder · Franke Landscape Architects

Open Spaces at Sandtorkai, HafenCity Hamburg

Through a collaboration between two generations of planners, this practice offers wide experience and innovative ideas for every aspect of open-space and landscape planning. Jens Bendfeldt (*1963) and Uli Franke (*1966) are graduate landscape architects and have been practice partners since 1995. Klaus Schröder (*1946) – working in the practice since 1973 and a partner since 1979 – is also landscape architect.

Hamburg   Eight pronounced solitary buildings, realised on the basis of competitions, between the street Am Sandtorkai opposite the Speicherstadt with its storage-buildings and the Sandtor harbour form the start of the development of the HafenCity Hamburg. Having the motto "Growing City", a new urban district is being created here in an incomparable location on the water in the city center. For flood protection, the buildings were erected on a polder construction that is used as a garage and whose roof between the buildings can be driven on by the emergency services during a flood. I The polder wall coverings, comprising large concrete parts and a dark blue clinker plug as material and colour-neutral foundation, looks powerful and reserved at the same time between the solitary buildings. A slight incline of the walls facing the water optically reduces the tilt of the relatively narrow quay promenade along the harbour. Together with the play of light and shade of the buildings rising above the promenade, steps with seating areas give the entire length of the polder a rhythm. The public quay promenade with the historic quay wall leads along the future traditional ships' harbour at Sandtorkai to the Magellan-Terraces of the harbour head. I The materials used, poured asphalt, wood, steel and clinker on the polder and large used granite stones and large concrete plates on the promenade reflect the harbour character and create a link to the harbour's former use and to the Speicherstadt.

above:
Old and new: attractive views
of the Speicherstadt
below:
Western quay promenade with
Construction Areas 1 to 5

Project Facts
Builder-owner: Free and Hanseatic City of Hamburg,
represented by HafenCity Hamburg GmbH (quay promenade),
Drees & Sommer GmbH, Plusbau GmbH, Wernst Immobilien AG, Bau-
Verein zu Hamburg, Aug. Prien GmbH, Cantina GmbH, DDS GmbH,
Quantum Immobilien AG (foundation)
Building Time: 2003–2005
Size: 6,600 m²
Architects: Ingenhoven und Partner, Böge Lindner, Spengler Wiescholek,
Schweger + Partner, Bothe Richter Teherani, Marc-Olivier Mathez, apb
Architects, Jan Störmer Architects (Sandtorkai), DHBT Architects
(seniors nursing home)

above left:
View from the seating steps
above right:
Evening atmosphere
below:
Stollers on the quay
promenade

above left:
"Nordish walking by nature"
above right:
quay promenade along historical quay wall
below:
Intersection and ground plan

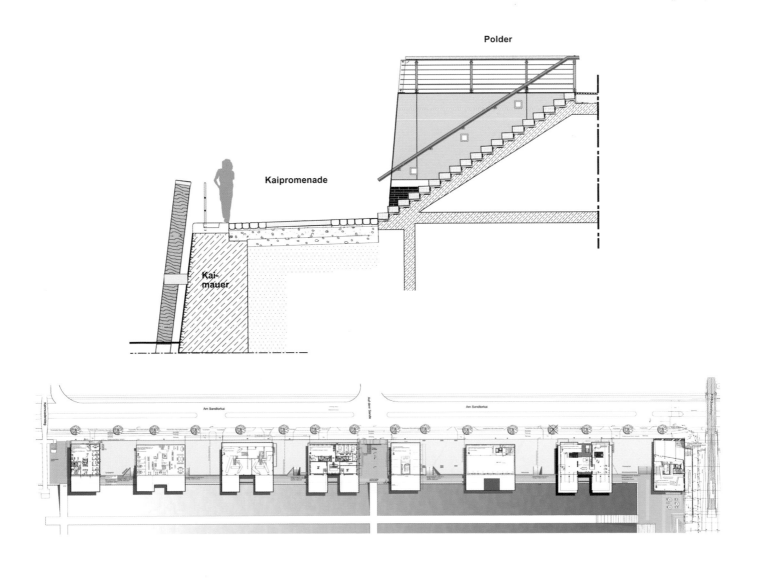

Polder

Kaipromenade

Kai-
mauer

Peter Walker and Partners

In 1983, Peter Walker founded the firm Peter Walker and Partners Landscape Architecture. Exploring the relationship between art and culture, PWP challenges traditional concepts of design. Their work results from knowledge of history and tradition, sympathy with contemporary needs, understanding of both conceptual and material processes, mastery of construction, and attention to detail.

Sony Center, Potsdamer Platz

Berlin   The Sony Center of Murphy/Jahn is an urban complex the size of an entire city block. It is composed of residential and office units, cultural centers and leisure facilities clustered around a central, ellipsoid plaza lined with restaurants and cafes. 35 metres above this central space a roof in the form of a glass and Teflon-coated fibreglass awning is supported by a slanting steel mast. The roof rises to a peak 62 metres above the ground and is the chief architectural element of the block. **I** The more than 100-metre long covered atrium, surrounded by its individual buildings of steel and glass, is the main design feature of the open space. Its central component is a pool cantilevered on one side and nestling within a half-moon shaped fringe of box hedge vegetation. The glass floor of the pool affords a glimpse of the cinema foyer on the lower level and from this underground foyer a spectacular view of the roof awning is available through the transparent surface. **I** The plaza floor is a mix of perforated metal plates and granite cobblestone. The main lines marked on the floor are a continuation of the architecture's lines on the exterior. Other lines of orientation are provided by diagonal lighting elements incorporated into the fine cobbling. The geometric pattern is underscored by a linear arrangement formed by rows of trees and stainless steel seating elements. **I** Unlike the graphic design of the plaza, which dispenses with natural references and uses only abstract forms, vegetation has been established outside the plaza, where it serves as a spatial demarcation. In a north easterly direction stands of lime trees point the way to the Tiergarten park.

above:
The cantilevered pool and curving box hedges frame a view of the subterranean movie theater
below:
An array of box hedges

Project Facts
Builder-owner: Sony Corporation
Building Time: 1999–2000
Size: 3 ha

above left:
Electroluminescent strips
provide a lighted paving
accent
above right:
The cantilevered pool
below left:
Site plan
below right:
Stainless-steel bollards

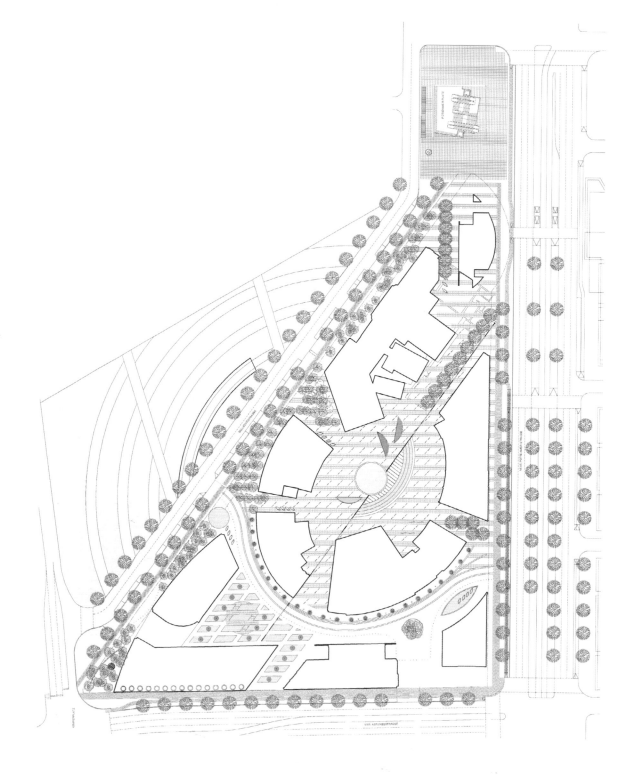

Thomanek + Duquesnoy

Beisheim-Center, Potsdamer Platz

Berlin   The perimeter grounds of the Beisheim Center are part of the overall planning of the individual complexes around Potsdamer Platz. The grounds have been configured to comply with one overarching principle governing the entire site: the individual architectural statement made by each area required the formulation of a unifying urban context. I The individual buildings of the Beisheim Center – by Hilmer + Sattler + Albrecht, Prof. Albers, David Chipperfield and Modersohn & Freiesleben – are classical Modern School in their architectural style. Motifs of this carry through into the design of the open areas. The exterior spaces are divided into private access roads used by the general public, a ground-level garden and the rooftop gardens of two hotels and flats. I Guiding principle in the design is the severe formality and geometric layout of the gardens, which decreases as we descend from the upper floors to the ground-floor garden. This diminishing degree of formality mirrors the increasing accessibility of the gardens: whilst hardly any of the rooftop gardens exist in more than an optical sense and cannot be enjoyed in their physical dimension, the large ground-floor garden can be used by the residents and people working in the vicinity. I Aside from the formal composition of the gardens the botanical concept underlines the garden character of the individual sections. The box tree is the basic vegetal type appearing in lines or as surface cover everywhere except for the roof gardens and the private thoroughfares. It is cultivated and trimmed as a wall or a physical body and so takes on the architectural quality of mass and density. The other aspect of the garden – its scenic quality, its colour and the softness of its contours – is established with the help of blossoming shrubs and bushes, selected trees and reed borders.

Developing clear concepts, adequate for the site in question – this is what Karl Thomanek and Hiltrud Duquesnoy aim to do. Putting their ideas into practice requires careful attention to detail, a selection of materials and plants to develop the sensuous aspect of the profession. With the great creative tradition of the discipline as a background they aim to find contemporary and sustainable solutions for the commissions they are set.

above:
Detail of fountain
below:
Large garden courtyard

Project Facts
Builder-owner: IMMAGO AG, Baar
Building Time: 2003
Size: 11,500 m²

above:
Varied views, private
roof garden, tenth floor
below:
Site plan

above right:
Roof garden of the Hotel
Marriott, third floor private roof
garden, tenth floor
below right:
Enclosure Auguste-Hauschner-
Strasse; fountain on the central
square

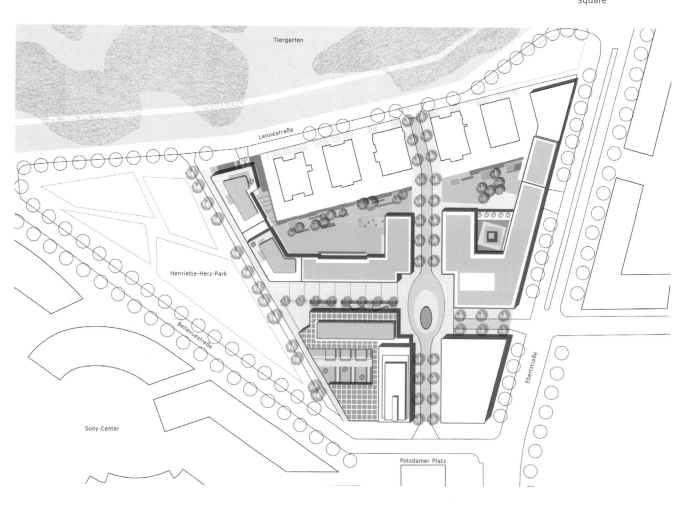

WES & Partners

The practice WES & Partners Landscape
Architects has been in existence for 36
years and is managed by Hinnerk
Wehberg, Peter Schatz, Wolfgang Betz
and Michael Kaschke. The tasks of the
practice cover the development of interi-
or and building architecture: open space
and project planning, the planning of
green spaces and landscapes, certificates
and urban planning projects as well as
building art.

Platz der Einheit

Postdam

The conventional approach to inner-city renewal is to create a peaceful inner-city area of green lawns. However, for the Platz der Einheit, the square in Potsdam dedicated to unifications the planners came up with an unusual architectural design for landscaping this urban space: towards the center of the square the large lawn areas were raised to create a deliberate declivity in the middle – the previously uninspiring flat grass area suddenly comes alive in a three-dimensional sense. I The raised lawn plateaus are bisected by two sunken diagonal paths which widen towards the point where they meet. This creates a kind of narrow pass, through which the visitor can walk between banks of roses and taxus. Alternatively, inward-facing steps offer the chance to sit down and enjoy a natural seclusion – the network of paths becomes a place to spend time that has its very own spatial atmosphere. This distinctly geometrical path design is a modern interpretation of a plan originated by Peter Joseph Lenné who, back in the nineteenth century, developed the square featuring a design in the form of a St. Andrew's cross. I The square's outer border consists of an arcade of lime trees. Its historical form has been augmented, while the planting of surface-covering shrubs and barrenwort, astilbes and geraniums, punctuated by anemone, cimicifuga and hosta, both accentuate and subdivide the space. The border is defined by a slatted gravel path all the way around. There are seats underneath the shadow of the trees between the flower beds. From here the visitor can observe all the hustle and bustle of the street adjacent to the square and watch people on the narrow pass as they descend into the green of the lawn – and disappear into the "sunken garden."

above:
View of the illuminated paths
in winter
below:
View of the square by day

Project Facts
Builder-owner: Sanierungsträger Potsdam,
Gesellschaft der behutsamen Stadterneuerung mbH
Building Time: 1997–1998
Size: 2.1 ha

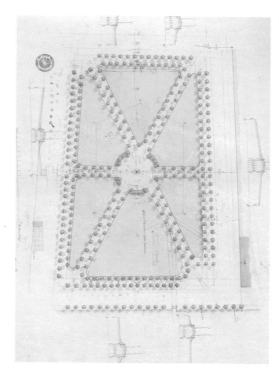

above left:
Snow-covered steps with "seat-
ed groups of plants"
above right:
Historical plan
below:
The crossroads as meeting place
right:
Site plan

BIERBAUM.AICHELE.landscape architects

The two landscape architects have been working together since 1996, covering all aspects of their profession – the firm was founded in 1980. Main attitude and starting point is the creation of high quality open spaces and landscapes. What is already there and what is perceived is set in new relationships and made visible; functions and contents are defined with the aim to access new spaces and to design sites that inspire.

Western Station Forecourt, Mainz Central Station

Mainz   In the course of modernisation work on Mainz Central Station, it was found necessary to make the station, previously accessible only on one side – from the city center to the east – also accessible from its rear side to the west. This provided an opportunity to enhance the environment there, that was considered unsatisfactory from a city-planning viewpoint, through new buildings and new uses. The aim of this new design was also to improve the quality of the site as a waiting area and to enhance its clarity, so that this inner-city site could be felt as an open space and offers the rail traveller an attractive reception and waiting zone. I A counterpart has been set to the busy, difficult conditions there by softly modelling the space by planting it uniformly with flowers across the whole area, making a grand and calming gesture. Rows of gleditsias and Eve Price in rows of lavender as well as a solitary paulownia create a Mediterranean atmosphere, surrounding the traveller with scent and colours in a spectacular way. The early flowering of the Eve Price gives way to the white and red of the tulips set between the rows of lavender, and from June onwards the purple panicles of the lavender and the yellow flowers of the sedium stay with the passers-by all through the summer. I The gleditsias, with their loose roof of foliage, cast a light shade over the park benches in the waiting area in front of the west entrance. In autumn and winter, too, the clear structures of the pruned rows of lavender, with the evergreen Eve Price, present an attractive and well-formed picture. A harmonious colour and lighting design, using modern reflector lights, gives the whole exterior zone a scenic framework, while contributing to the security of the station area.

above:
The softly modelled site, with lavender planted over all surfaces, creates peace and order in an area flooded with traffic
below:
Gleditsias cast light shadows across rows of lavender, creating an attractive reception and waiting area with a Mediterranean atmosphere

Project Facts
Builder-owner: Wirtschaftsbetrieb Mainz, Betriebszweig Strassen
Building Time: 2002
Size: 7,100 m²

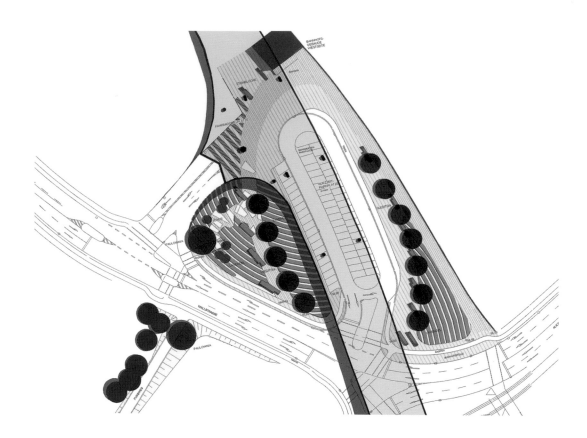

above left:
Plan
above right:
A softly-modelled design and uniform selection of plants has created an attractive spot, where it is a pleasure to stop for a while
below left:
Passers by and travellers are surprised by the Mediterranean atmosphere of the site, in the very center of the city
below right:
White and red tulips between the rows of lavender set the colours in spring

above:
Constructional context
(southern view)
below:
The design
right:
Views and perspectives

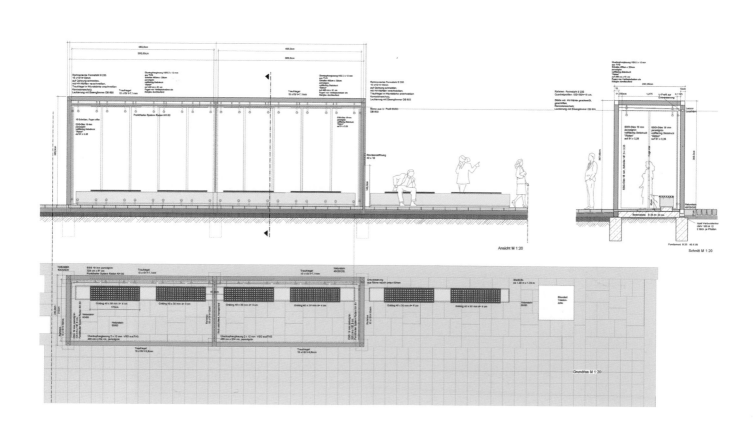

Peter Kluska

Peter Kluska, a trained gardener and freelance landscape architect, founded his
own practice in 1970. He defines his
method of work in the following way:
"My objective is to develop spatial compositions and design qualities which attain a
high level of implicitness, which are right
for the respective locations, which reach
people to satisfy their needs for usage and
for experience, create a good mood and
also carry a musical component."

Redesigning the Kabinettsgarten, Residenz Munich

Munich

A well known feature of Munich's Old Town are its many squares, courtyards and gardens. To the north, a series of gardens – Englischer Garten, Hofgarten and Kabinettsgarten – links the banks of the Isar with the city. After many years of neglect, the Kabinetts-garten, standing within the impressive architecture of the Residency in the very center of the city, has been redesigned in a way which is both contemporary and suitable to the site. This renovation was prompted by the remodelling of the adjoining Allerheiligen Hof-kirche to make a cultural event area. I Shallow ponds form the center of the garden. By analogy with an artificial flowerbed, green, red and white strips of glass mosaic sparkle on the dark green bottom of the basins (orthoquartzite). This colour composition is supplemented by plants in tubs, featuring blue-flow-ering agapanthus (blue lily). Via the central path the visitor reaches a square with four pruned plane trees and a round fountain. I With the aim of creating a light and bright garden, chalk and shell limestone have been used to reflect the warm colours of the Residency. The plants were selected to represent ele-ments of a classical garden. This includes two lime trees, four plane trees, whose tops have been pruned to form a cube-shaped roof, white-blooming magno-lias, high-growing scented rose trees, blossoming shrubs, beech hedges, and plants in pots along the ponds. An aura of evening festiveness is provided by slim, low lighting pillars and reflected light on the facades. The garden is for public use, and also serves as a foyer for cultural events in the Residency.

above:
Shallow water with glass
mosaic
below:
Concert interval in the garden

Project Facts
Builder-owner: Bavarian State Ministry of Finance,
represented by the Bavarian Administration of State Castles and Lakes
Building Time: 2002–2003
Size: 1,000 m²

above left:
Water-garden-
architecture (detail)
right:
Site plan

below left:
Garden in evening light

Charlottenzimmertrakt

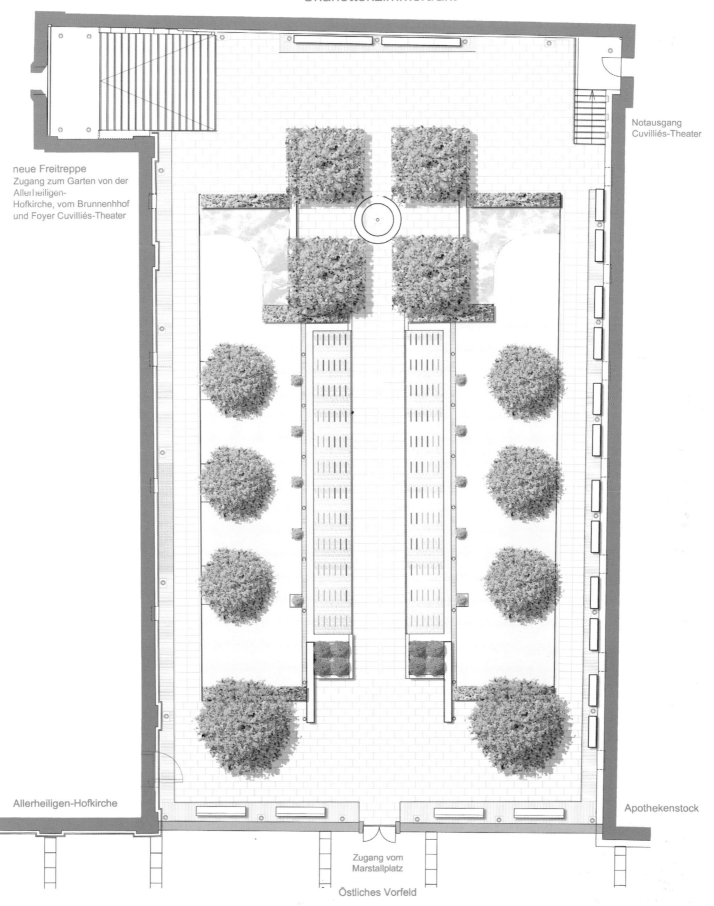

neue Freitreppe
Zugang zum Garten von der
Allerheiligen-
Hofkirche, vom Brunnenhhof
und Foyer Cuvilliés-Theater

Notausgang
Cuvilliés-Theater

Allerheiligen-Hofkirche

Apothekenstock

Zugang vom
Marstallplatz

Östliches Vorfeld

Burger Landscape Architects

Bayerforum – Holzkirchen Station Square

Munich

The realignment of the Holzkirchen railway station created a small independent forecourt, in conjunction with the construction of a new administrative building. Its design enables it to convey a peaceful atmosphere, within a busy location. I The inward-looking site of the "vertical garden" is counterbalanced by the raised zone of the "tree square", providing an extended waiting area for streetcars, and serving as a visual focus and marker to the entrance for the whole square. An integral part of the design is a fountain, composed of a horizontal and a vertical level, which complement each other in their materials and dimensions. A curved wall with a long bench closes off the area from the street. The supporting wall, which cushions the sharp rise between the street level and the level of the underpass, forms the vertical section of the fountain. Window-like embrasures have been let into the travertine surface, which are filled in with quarry stone of Theuma shale. Ferns and mosses will grow into the joints over the years, covering the stones with a soft green. I The actual fountain is in front of the wall. Large slabs of natural stone and stainless steel are placed in a free sequence and bisected by water channels like a carpet in front of the fountain wall. The wide variety of materials and sequential levels of the fountain create a changing play of colour. The special shape of the channels means that the noise of the water can be heard all the time, as it flows constantly.

Susanne Burger (*1961), a trained ceramic designer and graduate landscape architect, worked from 1995 in her own practice. In all the planning she undertakes her main focus is on an unambiguous formulation of a design theme, always linked with an empirical definition of space. Her design work concentrates on a clear formal language, expressed in memorable use of materials and sharpness of detail.

above:
Square of trees and fountain
below:
The fountain wall

Project Facts
Builder-owner: GVG, Munich
Building Time: 1999–2000
Size: 1,950 m²

above left:
Isometry
above right:
Seating bench at the fountain
(detail); materiality of the
fountain slabs

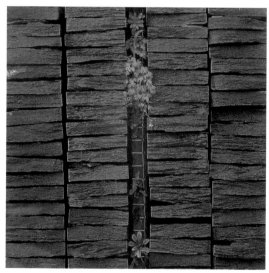

below left:
Fountain system (details)
below right:
Design plan

Rainer Schmidt Landscape Architects

Square in Front of the Bavarian National Museum

Munich   For the project to redesign the forecourt of the Bavarian National Museum the idea of a sunken forum, a major feature of the forecourt in the early years of the 20th century, was resurrected and given a fresh interpretation. The notion of enlarging and designing a space using the Forum as one of the design features has not changed with the years. I Instead of the original neo-baroque formality associated with ornamental foliage, curving lines and topiary cones, today's Forum has clear lines and geometry. In a deliberate borrowing from baroque design skewed-angle levels were created to alter spatial perceptions and create new ones. The forecourt's key design element is the Forum's reconciling of aesthetic and functional imperatives: it serves as a place for visitors to spend time, thereby injecting new life into the area. Lined on two sides with wide walls of granite the Forum descends from the street towards the main entrance, ending in a broad staircase. Top quality materials abound in the new raised garden. The dark green of the wedge-shaped box hedge is in stark contrast to the white strips of quartzite cobbles and the lawn verges with their stainless steel edges. The Forum is bordered by an area decked in a carpet-like covering of wide and narrow strips. The wide strips are yellow granite slabs; the narrower strips make use of the existing, dark grey granite. I The surface of the forecourt has been enhanced with the addition of two stands of magnolias and after nightfall a system of illuminations highlights the major design elements: LED strips in the steps create a floating effect, ground-level spotlights focus on the trees and the illuminated facade provides an attractive backdrop to the newly designed forecourt.

Project Facts
Builder-owner: Circle of Friends of the Bavarian National Museum, represented by Argenta Anlagengesellschaft mbH
Building Time: 2002–2005
Size: 4,000 m²

The philosophy of the business, founded in 1991, is to find answers to the problems of our times, aware that the landscape architecture of the twenty-first century should be a realistic reflection of how people come to terms with each other and with nature. Rainer Schmidt attempts to realise these answers in designs, thus finding a balance between design, functions and feelings.

above:
The forum, with linearity and geometry, unites aesthetic and functional needs
below:
The new design of the square takes its inspiration from the historical design, interpreting it in a new way

above and mid left:
Visualisation of the forecourt
in the design stage
above right:
Wedge-shaped beech hedges
form a strong contrast to the
white pavement strips and the
lawns

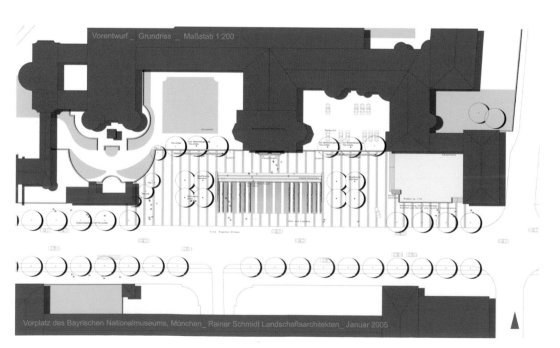

below left:
Design drawing for the
forecourt
below right:
The Forum runs gently down
towards the main gate with an
open-air staircase

Christophe Girot

Christophe Girot studied environmental planning and management at the University of California in Davis as well as architecture and landscape architecture at Berkeley. Since 1999 he has been professor of Landscape Architecture at the ETH and recently founded the Institute of Landscape Architecture, ETH Zurich. Since 1986 he has been a partner in several offices in France and Switzerland. In 2005 he founded Atelier Girot in Zurich.

Invalidenpark

Berlin   Today's Invalidenpark lies in an area developed in the middle of the eighteenth century by disabled Prussian soldiers for agricultural use and was destroyed in the Second World War – due to the partition of the city, the ruined buildings had to be removed for the adjoining border installations. | After Reunification, the intention was to redefine a new identity for the area – with this challenge that this project must not only confront a particular moment in history, but must cope with a series of historical developments. The design aims to make former structures visible, and at the same time create a distance from them, in order to convey a new and contemporary message. | The result is a clear, two-part design, avoiding historical reconstructions and skilfully combining an urban square with a landscape park. This combination is brought about by narrow strips of grass, which begin in the granite covering of the square, and broaden out step by step towards the park. This paving is interrupted by a rectangular water basin. The visitor can climb along the top of a wall above the basin, thus providing a certain distance from the site's problematic past. | The ascent begins with a path which exposes a strip of the historical foundation walls of the Gnadenkirche, thus displaying in the ground a record of the past landscape. The wall sculpture, named by journalists "Trail to the Future", runs ramp-like to a height of over seven metres. Instead of taking your bearings from the former Prussian central axis of the park, water basin and wall are set in a north-south direction – this partition between East and West is a reminder of Germany's history. Ginkgos are planted on the square in lines – an ancient symbol of hope and determination.

above:
View of the urban square along the Invalidenstrasse
below:
Ramp and way as an extension of the foundation of the church

Project Facts
Builder-owner: Grün Berlin Park und Garten GmbH
Building Time: 1992–1997
Size: 2.5 ha

left above:
View of the side paths from the back of the park towards Invalidenstrasse
left below:
View of the wall and its reflection in the water basin – illuminated at night
right above:
View of the urban square at the front of the park
right mid:
View of the children's park at the back of the park
right below:
Water fall at the edge of the wall

DS landscape architects

Tilla-Durieux-Park / Henriette-Herz-Park, Potsdamer Platz

Berlin
These two parks, adjoining Potsdamer Platz, designed in collaboration with the landscape architect Thomas M. Dietrich, must be seen as an overall plan, jointly forming a link between the Tiergarten and the green area planned on the old "Railway Triangle" (Gleisdreieck). I The park, named after the Austrian actress and resistance activist Tilla Durieux, forms a counterpoint to the new buildings in the Quartier DaimlerChrysler. It is less a park in the traditional sense, more a landscape sculpture, encouraging the spectator to perceive and to move in an unaccustomed way. The main section of lawn, 450 metres long, with banks of up to 4 metres high and downwards slopes of up to 35 degrees, has been turned on its longitudinal axis. A broad cutting in the midst of this lawn sculpture provides space for five oversize see-saws, which have been so positioned as to provide a playful counterpart in movement to the turned-in lawn. I The Henriette-Herz-Park is a metaphor for breaking up and coming together. A large lawn between the Sony-Center and the Beisheim-Center has been "broken up" into four sections. Narrow paths cross the angulated, clod-like sections of turf, creating an attractive spatial experience. The paths, edged in red Finnish granite, are a symbol of the breaks and changes of Berlin's history. This motif of tectonic faults and of motion regained between East and West was developed in collaboration with the Israeli artist Shlomo Koren. The green of the grass and the red of the stone edging and pavement give the place a characteristically peaceful and austere aspect.

The designs of DS landscape architects, founded in 1993, are a response to the dominant architecture of speed, offering architecture of deceleration as its poetic counterpart. They form new landscapes that stimulate the imagination by making a powerful choice for one atmosphere and ensuring clarity and simplicity in the form and application of material.

above:
A birds-eye view of the Tilla-Durieux-Park
mid:
Henriette-Herz-Park, view from the Sony-Center
below:
Evening ambiance in the Tilla-Durieux-Park

Project Facts
Builder-owner: District Office of Berlin-Mitte
Building Time: 2002–2003
Size: 2.5 ha (Tilla-Durieux-Park); 1 ha (Henriette-Herz-Park)

above left:
Passageway through
embankment
above right:
Five seasaws in the middle
of Tilla-Durieux-Park
below:
View of the Quartier
DaimlerChrysler at Potsdamer
Platz

above:
Lawn in Henriette-Herz-Park,
coloured in violet by crocuses
below:
Site plan

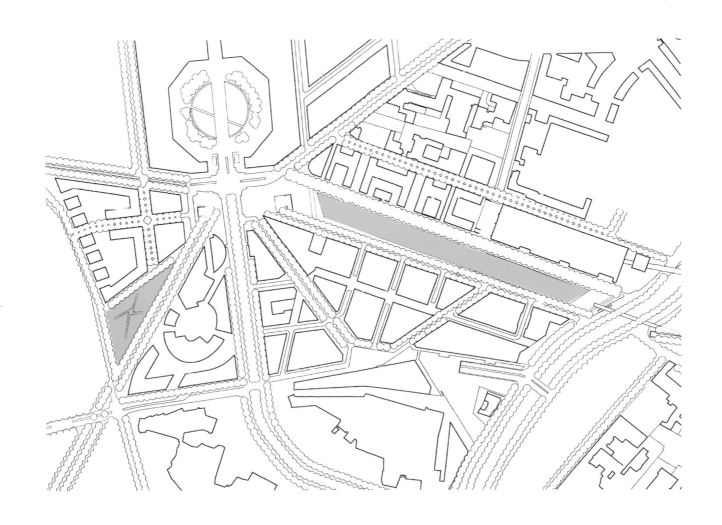

Hanke + Partners Landscape Architects

The practice was founded in 1981 by Reinhard Hanke. Barbara Hanker has been a partner since 1990, and Holger Plaasche since 1997. Prior to the foundation of the practice, these three partners were for long engaged on joint projects. In their practice they work on competitions and projects, focusing on site planning and landscape planning, and are engaged in the preparation of expert reports and in development commissions.

Green Space in Kaskelkiez

Berlin   A small park with a marked topography: Through the new design of the green area in the recently renovated Kaskelkiez in the Berlin district of Lichtenberg, a small but open and inviting park was created which re-interprets the location through its simple design. I Two rows of trees planted in blocks recall the former historic block development and now form the backdrop for the new park. The external contours of the park support the formation of space, developed walls stand in contrast to the interaction of the green edges of the lawned embankments. Continuing to the corner area, rising internal areas and walls give the entrance area a design accent; a generously proportioned staircase bridges the difference in height to the path. The lawns running parallel to the walls rise in the opposite direction and underline the edges of the space in their interaction to the walls in front of the edges. I Inside the park differently designed spaces have been created: a generous and open lawn with individual trees forms an open space which can be looked into. By lowering the lawn there is a clear edge which is lineated by a corten steel wall and gives the surrounding paths here a stair-like character. I In the inner part of the park there are two small play areas which can be made out from some distance by the colour of the materials used. Hedges form small niches around the play areas. Plate bands as small paths made from the same material and colour as the surrounding walls open up the play areas. Seating is provided by the gently distributed chairs at the end of the plate bands. The final points of these bands are designed as small constellations at night with pointed solar lights.

above:
Two playgrounds form an attraction for children and young people
below:
Hedges of prunus lauracerasus provide a structure for the northern section of the park

Project Facts
Builder-owner: State of Berlin,
represented by the District Office of Berlin-Lichtenberg
Building Time: 2004
Size: 2,700 m²

above left:
Solar lights in the paved strips
set a particular tone at night
above right:
The topography supports the
spatial design
below left:
Site plan
below right:
Chairs set loosely apart
provide somewhere to sit;
colourful surfaces accentuate
the playgrounds

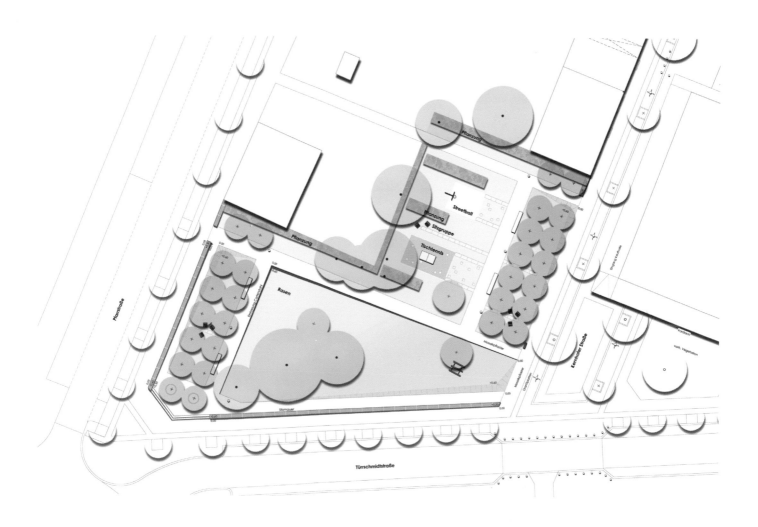

Gruppe F Landschaftsarchitektur Freiräume

To create landscape – in urban as well as rural spaces – stands for the landscape architects of Gruppe F (group F) for the creation of spaces to develop new possibilities. This created scopes for development encourage fantasy and creativity, without claiming a clear benefit. For the group concept and planning are interactive processes for those involved.

Grassland Park on the River Wuhle and Municipal Gardens

Berlin   The Grassland Park on the river Wuhle and the associated Municipal Gardens are situated on the periphery of Berlin and are part of an all-embracing green swathe running between large housing developments of the socialist period. With the rebuilding of the Landsberger Tor district, it became necessary to develop the green swathe further and to design a park for the district. I The Municipal Gardens run through the residential area as a narrow strip of undulating grass, with a space-defining purpose. Recreational areas have been incorporated into the striking, 400 metre long ground design, as if moulded into the terrain. Clear demarcation of the dynamic topography – and consequent designation of the grassy undulations as a ground sculpture – is created by a concrete wall. Vegetation marks the qualities of individual spots: groups of shrubs "dance" with the undulating grass, trees in cubic configurations define urban areas, groves provide allusions to the surrounding countryside. A main feature of the central square is that of outside furniture specially developed for this project: revolving chairs, benches and waste-paper baskets are transformed into parts of a landscape-architecture design. I In planning the Grassland Park, the aim was to provide the edge of the city with its own design by developing strong landscape structures which would deliberately highlight the hybrid nature of this area – no longer country, but not yet urbanised – emphasising its position on the edge of the city. In its spacious width, the new park provides an exciting mixture of unspoiled countryside, man-made adjuncts, and urban elements. I The main features of the broad grassland area, with its unpretentious vegetal spatiality, are individual groups of trees, sparing provision of paths, and so-called "loci spectabilis."

above:
"Loci spectabilis":
rain-retention reservoir
mid:
The rust-red balconies
in the outskirts of the city
below:
"Loci spectabilis": the
tamarisk grove

Project Facts
Builder-owner: ELT, ARGE Marzahn
Building Time: 1998–2002
Size: 18.5 ha

above left:
Play venues: "Wiesentraum",
young people's sports area
above right:
"The blue Wuhl in the sea of
grass"
below:
Site plan

above left:
Shrub garden
above right:
"Loci" in the
Municipal Gardens

below left:
400 metre wave:
the Municipal Gardens
below right:
Transition from the Municipal
Gardens to the Grasslands Park

Därr Landscape Architects

Vineyard Meadows

Halle / Saale

The new Heide-Süd city district, containing residential accommodation, a science and innovation park, and the new campus of the Martin Luther University, was built on the site of a former Soviet garrison, after the troops had pulled out. To provide a link between Halle-Neustadt and this new city district, a public open space was created, averaging 100 metres in width, stretching from east to west. Because of its spacious unspoiled meadows and a former adjoining vineyard, it was named Vineyard Meadows. This development is a major part of a green system for the whole city, linking further local recreational areas with the center. | Designing Vineyard Meadows as a public park has created a clear architectural space, a green backbone providing orientation and identity, and anchoring the adjoining building developments in the city. Its main ecological components are an improvement in the fresh air channelled to the neighbouring housing developments, a well-developed system for utilising rainwater, and the preservation and creation of specific living spaces for the local fauna. The rehabilitation of the abandoned site has not left any adaptable historical remnants in the original. However, rescued granite kerbs, piled up as dry walls and arranged as stele walls, are used as a clear and strong design feature. | Prescribed functions and décor elements, concentrated on a few selected points, were agreed with young users, street workers and social planners, to achieve as high a degree of acceptance as possible.

Därr Landscape Architects, set up in July 1990, works on every content in the field of open space planning. This demands a comprehensive thinking which influences the realisation of extensive plannings and the integration of object planning in a positive way. Within many objects the practice deals with the open space planning of parks and playgrounds as well as hospitals etc.

above:
Park access on the
Grimmritzer Damm
below:
Area of miscanthus in autumn

Project Facts
Builder-owner: City of Halle / Saale,
represented by Sachsen-Anhaltinische
Landesentwicklungsgesellschaft mbH (SALEG)
Building Time: 1999–2001
Size: approx. 20 ha

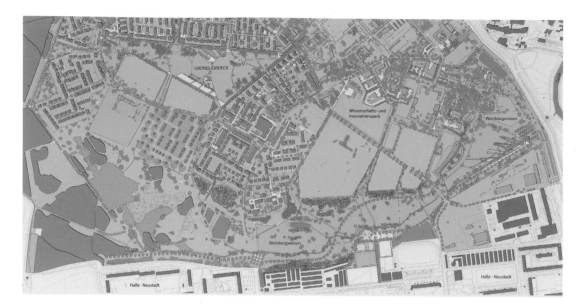

above left:
Heide South master plan
above right:
Gardens and terraces on the
future stream bed

below left:
Former tank-washing
installation, now back to
nature
below right:
Old granite road kerbs used to
create a stele

Häfner / Jiménez

The philosophy of the planning team of Häfner / Jiménez is reflected in its projects and competition entries: the omnipresent deluge of stimuli are confronted by living spaces oriented towards clarity and order. Developments are created which can be maintained at low commercial cost; they are using planning approaches which are both precise and suitable for the site and never missing a certain generosity.

Green Arch Paunsdorf

Leipzig

The Bürgerpark terrace and the former military exercise site of the Heiterblick barracks are the first part of the development known as the Grüner Bogen – Green Arch – Paunsdorf, part of the Leipzig's largest outdoor development. On one hand, the area is to become a recreational area for the residents of the neighbouring high-rise development, but the space is also to be a protected living space for animals, some of which are threatened with extinction. The two requirements were unified by means of landscape architecture and innovative natural protection planning to form a model solution. The project was accompanied by Dr. Trude Poser and Partners Landscape Ecology and Landscape Planning. I The idea of the "Green Arch" was strengthened in order for this important city-planning and landscaped element to become a generous green area on the outskirts of Leipzig. A parcours surrounding the entire residential estate forms the boundary between city and open landscape. It is portrayed by a system of two paths: a 4 metre-wide asphalt path is available for fast traffic. This is accompanied by a path with a waterbound cover for more gentle traffic. I The basic structure of the public space is based on the interaction between dense urban space, with squares and promenades, and the open landscape park. The terraces, located at the junctions of the parcours and topographically formed into viewing platforms, play an important role here in defining the cityscape. Trees reinforce the continuity of the parcours and form a binding element. I On the approximately 35 ha military exercise site as the largest part of the landscape park, the pastures are used all year round by cattle and Przewalski horses. These attractiv animals increase the experience in the Green Arch Paunsdorf. A path around the entire pasture site, which is built as a construction of wood and steel in sensitive areas to protect the fauna, envelopes the site.

above:
The show-jumping course is the dividing line
mid:
The terrace during the opening
below:
Visitors on the terrace

Project Facts
Builder-owner: City of Leipzig, Green Spaces Office
Building Time: 2003–2004
Size: 41.2 ha

above:
The terrace – an overview
below:
Site plans;
Impressions

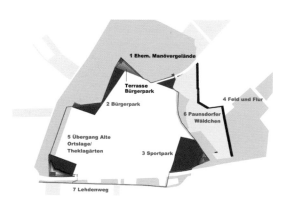

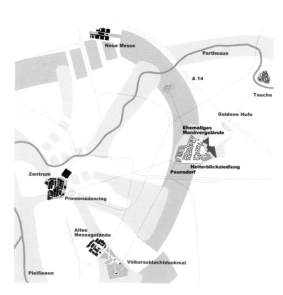

above:
View from the terrace to the
Municipal Park, planned
below:
Paunsdorf green belt,
overall plan

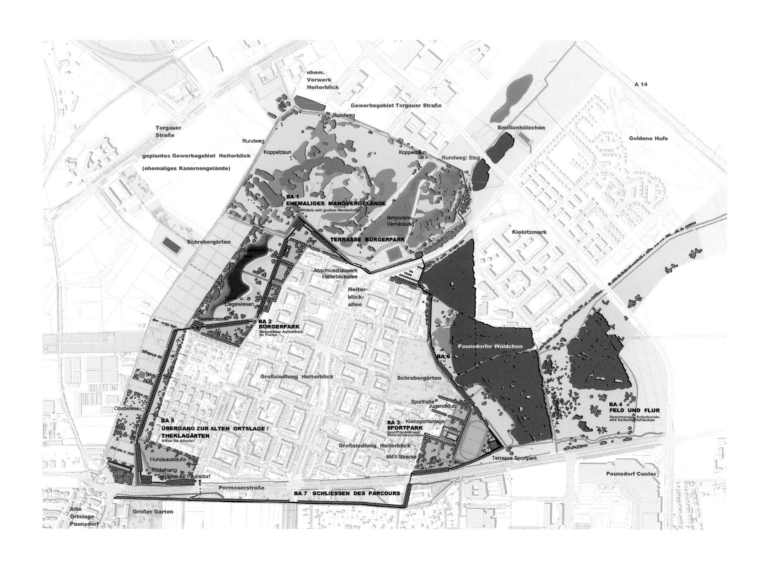

BIERBAUM.AICHELE.landscape architects

The two landscape architects have been working together since 1996, covering all aspects of their profession – the firm was founded in 1980. Main attitude and starting point is the creation of high quality open spaces and landscapes. What is already there and what is perceived is set in new relationships and made visible; functions and contents are defined with the aim to access new spaces and to design sites that inspire.

Heidenfahrt Rhine Bank

Heidesheim

As part of a project entitled "A region in dialogue – developing and planning the meadow banks of the Rhine between Mainz and Ingelheim", since 1997 plans have been drawn up, in collaboration with local people, to provide a series of guides for the future development of this landscape. One of three key projects in this model was to settle the design of the Heidenfahrt Rhine Bank and to carry it out in two construction stages. I Areas formerly used as a car park or camping ground have been made into promenades, seating and sun-bathing areas by the water. The permanent camping ground, which earlier sealed off the bank, has been converted into a seasonal camping ground, which makes it possible to have a through public path along the bank once more. Next to the newly designed jetty for small passenger boats comes a section of the bank some 300 metres long, running to the old Rhine estuary, on which a model natural restoration of the Rhine bank has been carried out: stone embankments and coverings have been removed, and the bank flattened out. A flood basin along the summer dyke has been further laid out as a fosse. I To improve high-water retention, some 10,000 m³ of earth has been removed from the flood area. The fosse, which up till now flowed almost invisibly into the Rhine through piping, has been redesigned in a natural way, so that the estuary area can now be enjoyed with its changing Rhine water levels. I The transition from the dyked meadow to the recent one, where roads meet from five different directions, is now marked by a new bastion. Earlier this area was used only as a dyke crossing; now the small square on the bastion, topped by a summer lime tree, is the central meeting place and viewing point for this section of the river bank. Paths lead from the bastion to the promenade and across the new fosse bridge to the landing stage, which is shadowed by lime trees in roof-like rows.

above:
The new bastion is the central meeting and observation point
below:
Today a bridge replaces the former pipe outlet

Project Facts
Builder-owner:
Ministry of Environment and Forestry of the State Rhineland-Palatinate
Building Time: 2002–2004
Size: approx. 6 ha
Expert Adviser: Ruiz Rodriguez + Zeisler, Ingenieurgemeinschaft für Wasserbau und Wasserwirtschaft

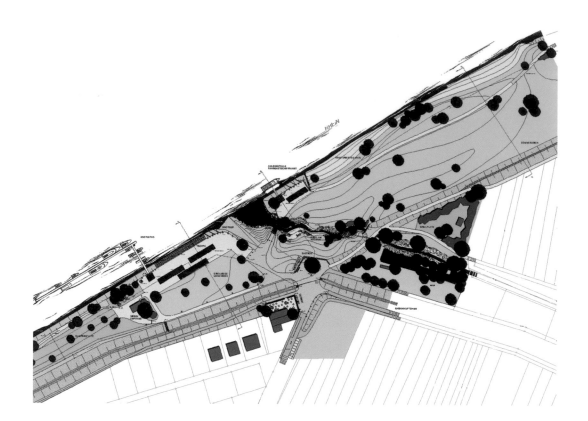

above left:
Site plan, design
above right:
The new Rhine promenade:
seats under a roof of lime
trees

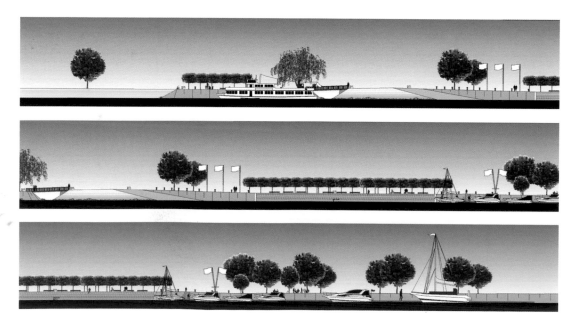

below left:
View of river banks, design
below right:
The lighting bollards (an extra
design) mark the line of the
bank

Werkgemeinschaft Freiraum

South City Park Fürth

Fürth   The South City Park in Fürth is situated on the site of former barracks with existing buildings from different periods and a stock of old trees. The main objectives when considering future use of the site were reorganisation and integration into the city – along with developing a residential and mixed area. This involved laying out a park close to the inner city, to serve as a linking element with the adjacent areas. I With its simple rectangular shape, the park picks up the original, austere organisation of the former barracks location. Geometrical areas divide the site clearly into three parts. Broad, lowered lawns are framed by a promenade, which is crossed by a three-row avenue – this compact framework of 350 lime trees forms the backbone of the park, creating a spatial border. The area is linked on all sides with its neighbouring areas, and the promenade is linked via the two playgrounds to west and east with the adjoining residential districts – thus integrating it with the urban environment. I In contrast to the severe geometry of the lime-tree promenade, flowering cherries are distributed across the open squares in a loose arrangement; the paving there is of shaped natural stone, taken from the former barrack roadways. Two transverse fountains emphasise the links with the surrounding city. On the Stadtplatz East the difference in height from the park to the street has been used to create steps and waterfalls; on the Stadtplatz West an illuminated wall with green overgrowth forms a background for sunny seats by the fountain. I Beneath its well-designed surface, the park conceals a particular technical feature: all lawns, trees and hedges are equipped with automatic watering devices, supplied from a cistern which is filled by ground water.

WGF develops projects in all sizes for single objects, cities and regions, in the fileds of planning, moderation, teaching and basic innovations. The orders are often aquired through competitions. Rewards like the Deutsche Städtebaupreis 1993, the Deubau-Bauherrenpreis 1996 or the Deutsche Landschaftsarchitekturpreis 1997 and 2005 confirm the continuous development over more than 30 years.

above:
Playhill-landscape
mid:
The playhill-landscape as part of the promenade
below:
View of the promenade

Project Facts
Builder-owner: City of Fürth
Building Time: 2001–2004
Size: 9.5 ha
Design play elements: Prof. Aufmkolk and Manuela Scheuerer, Landscape Architect, Fürth; Florian Aigner
Further Participants: pesch partner, architects urban planners herdecke

101

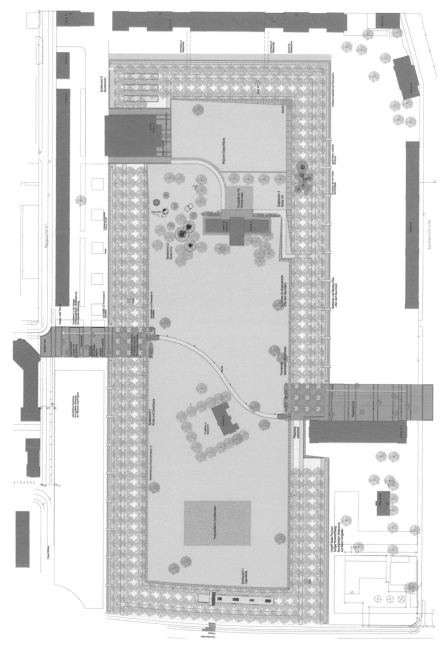

above left:
Living with a view of the park
above right:
Play-art by Monica Gora
below:
Site plan

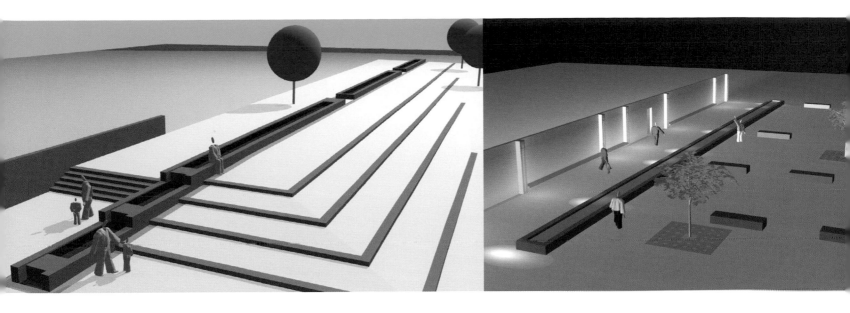

above left:
Stadtplatz East
above right:
Stadtplatz West
below:
Overview as isometry

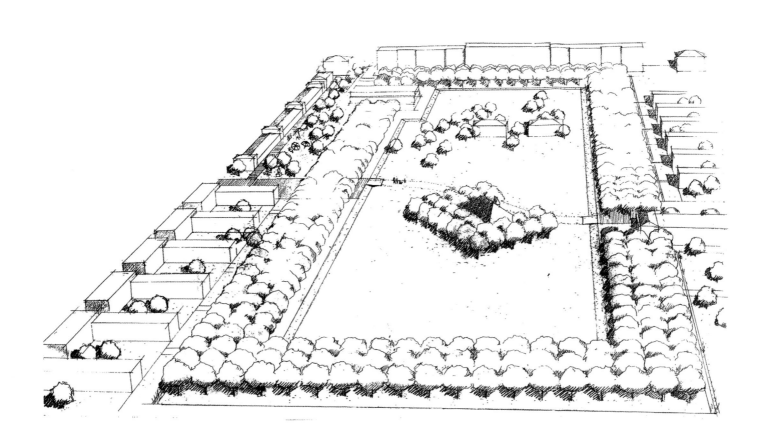

Levin Monsigny Landscape Architects

Redesigning the Georg-Freundorfer-Platz

Munich   The square Georg-Freundorfer-Platz lies in Munich's Westend district, a working-class area dating from the second half of the 19th century, built on the ribbon-block principle. Further housing development is taking place on the adjoining Theresienhöhe, formerly a fair and exhibition center. The Georg-Freundorfer-Platz has an important function in the urban context: it serves as a meeting place for the people living there, as an event venue, and as a multifunctional area, where people can play and sit. **I** Laid out with grass as early as the 1960s, high earthen walls, overgrown with woody vegetation, form a barrier between the city district and the square. It was necessary for the redesign both to incorporate the existing trees – and thus also the banks – and to recreate the square's lost link with the city. To combine the area into a unity, after it had been divided up by different design features and the requirements of different usage, the Georg-Freundorfer-Platz was given a design and functional framework to provide an organising feature for opening up the area. **I** The frame is accentuated by a fine, bright "decorative ridge." It runs along the ground, dividing the dark basalt surface into a wide section of small paving stones and a narrow strip of mosaic. The ridge rises upwards and becomes an item of furniture, from which one is able to view the lively bustle taking place on the square. Integrated lighting strips follow its rhythm, making the regained size of the square clearly perceivable in the evening too. **I** On the frame are placed modelled mounds of vegetation, defining individual thoroughfares in the northern section of the square, and becoming smaller and lower to the south towards the Theresienplatz, until they are no more than green tufts, projecting from the dark natural stone of the frame. On entering the square, beneath the protective roof of the trees and between the lush beds of shade-loving ground shrubs, both passers by and people living in the area will find grasses and ferns.

This international practice, founded in 1998, is run by Martina Levin, Luc Monsigny, Nicolai Levin and Axel Hermening. The basis of each design is a precise analysis of the site in its environment and an optimum organisation of task and functions. In their work together they direct intensive thought to the most fundamental material which the landscape architect has at his disposal – the plant.

above:
The bright bench line accentuates the dark basalt surface of the development's framework-
below:
The spatial concentration of all installations leaves large open spaces free

Project Facts
Builder-owner: State Capital of Munich, Department of Horticulture
Building Time: 2001–2002
Size: 1.8 ha
Site Management:
Hubert Wendler Practice, Munich

above left:
Bands of light demonstrate
the size of the square at night.
above right:
The framework of the development creatively combines the
different functional areas into
a unity.

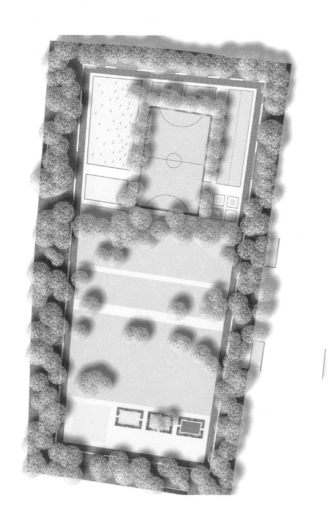

below left:
The individual design levels
emphasise the clarity of the
conception.
below right:
Alternation between light and
dark materials is the main feature of the square.

realgrün Landscape Architects

Arnulfpark

Munich

The revitalisation of a former railway container station between the Donnersberger Brücke and the Hackerbrücke has created a new city district, close to the center in an exposed position, with 850 residential units, plus office and commercial premises. A central element in this urban design is a large inner park, measuring 80 by 500 metres, which runs through the new district, making a permanent effect on the quality of life there. I The new park is being built at an aggregation point of so-called "fluxes", which relate to the lines of movement in the surroundings – both actual and potential – thus integrating them into the park. The streams of traffic for the railway are bundled towards the station; building developments become denser towards the city center. The ecologically valuable edges to the railway ballast lines, with their spontaneous vegetation of beeches and robinias, are compressed into an ecological corridor. The basic theme of the design – an interpretation of the site as an aggregation of different movements, streams and relationships vis-à-vis the inner city – is well expressed in the transformation of the typical "wild" arborial vegetation accompanying the railway into a self-aggregating, "cultivated" grid plantation of an inner-city kind. Interruptions and anomalies in this largely urban texture are created by nuanced topographical elevations to the lawns. The dynamic appearance of the park is characterised by flowing sectional areas, which come together to form a holistic appearance. I The model of a bright park, flooded with light, determined the selection of trees and the materials used for surfacing and installations.

In their work the planners are committed to an analytical and systematic methodology of design; landscape architecture is the result of an intellectual process, not the result of applying individualistic canons of form and material as a recipe. This process starts from an analysis of the task and the site, and its method is to progress via a clear concept to an appropriate draft solution.

above:
To the west of the park, in the garden flux, is a play area for children, featuring sand pits, a large umbrella for shade, seats and play accessories
below:
The play hill, covered with a light-beige fall-cushioning surface, becomes a steep mountain face; bubble seats of white concrete and a climbing rope complete the playground

Project Facts
Builder-owner: Vivico Real Estate, Subsidiary Munich
Building Time: 2004–2005
Size: 3.9 ha

above right:
The new park is being built at an aggregation point of highly disparate fluxes. The commanding flows of movement react to outer influences. Irritation produces reaction: deflection and topography

below left:
The play flux lies at the center of the park, with a view of the generation plant – a spacious play and adventure area, equipped in a wide variety of ways

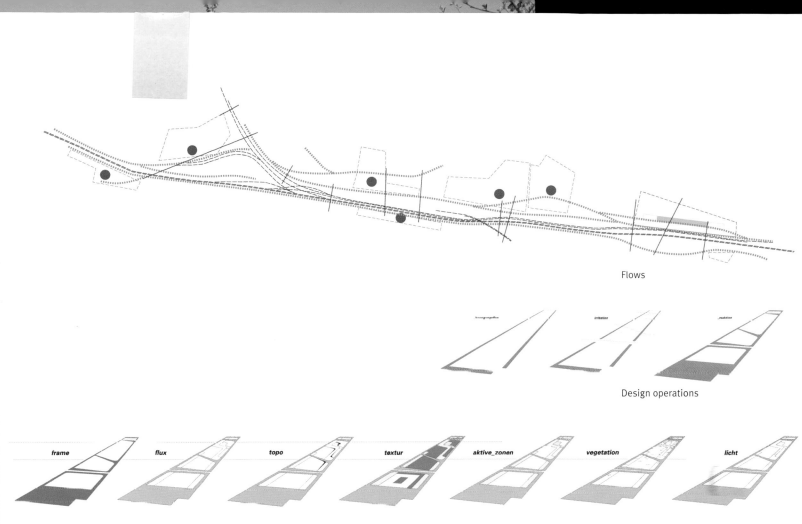

Flows

Design operations

frame *flux* *topo* *textur* *aktive_zonen* *vegetation* *licht*

Design layer

● *lärche* ● *kirsche* ○ *gleditschie*

Distribution and density of the trees

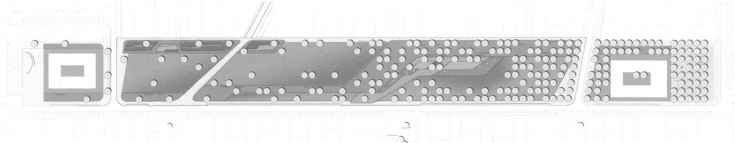

Site plan

Petuelpark

Munich   In 1996 Munich
tral ring road M
nelling into thre
ings. In the area
few link roads,
the tunnel, which
of Schwabing
urban repair usi
ture. I Planning
requirements: t
metres long, on
featuring a quit
the jump in heig
gitudinally into
tunnel and the v
Kanal is designe
calm retreat. Th
areas and recre
forms the active
component in
Village and Engl
and of the nort
and Luitpoldpa
instead of a sea
is particularly s
same time, wit
and naturally re
facilities for rec
this park desig
curator, develop
part of QUIVID,
programme. Or
the arts is a ca
the Lehnbachh
park and 13 wo
ated a holistic
the arts domina

above left:
"Bedroom"
above right:
"Bathroom"
mid left:
Ramp arrangement on the
Pfennigparade
mid right:
Irispseudacorus forms the
edging of the Nymphenburg-
Biederstein Canal
below left:
Island with Roman Signer's
"Spraying Boots"
below right:
Climbing game in the play
environment

above left:
Aerial view, looking north
above right:
"Wall sofa" in the "living room"
below:
General plan

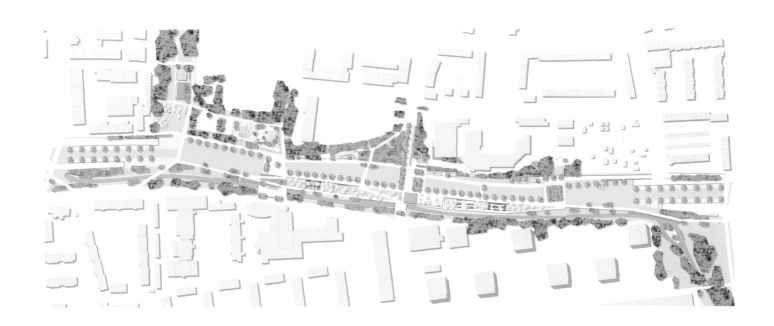

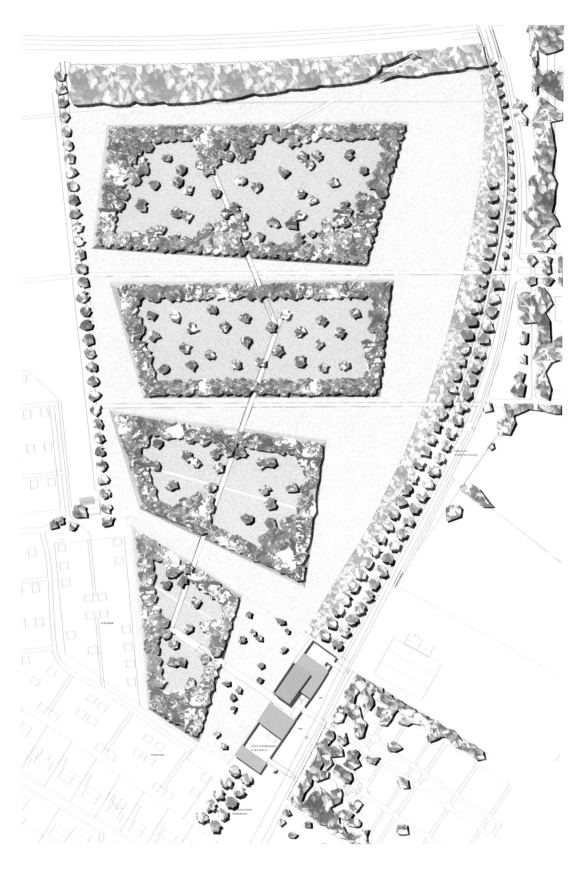

left:
Site plan
above right:
Approach in the direction of
the Hochkreuz (high crucifix)
by Hermann Biglmeyer;
Enclosure with dry wall
below right:
Urn wall;
Approach to burial place

above left:
Pond planted with water
irises
above right:
Detail of the meditation
garden with a view of the
meadows
below:
Plan of the cemetery

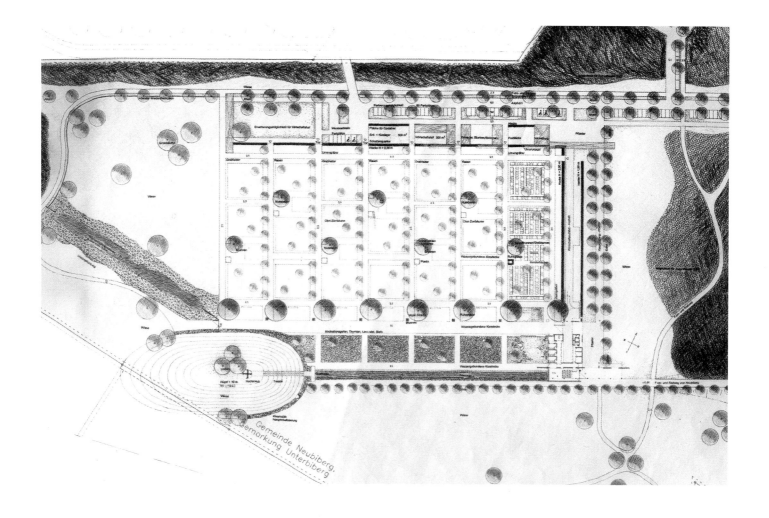

above left:
Urn-burial field with sand-
stone slabs and cross of grass
above right:
Detail of meditation garden
below:
View from the mortuary
chapel with pond and lookout

above left:
The Utoquai, uninterrupted by hedges and walls along the street, connects the city with the shore
below left:
Urbanistic concise road axis towards the lake at the lower lakeside in Zurich
right:
In the town house area high trees give the square with vista onto the lake its character

Planning Group DIPOL Landscape Architects / Christopher T. Hunziker

Wahlenpark

Zurich

The Wahlenpark is the last of four new parks to be established in Zurich as part of the development of the new district of Neu-Oerlikon. The park design is based on dividing the total area into three parts, using a colour scheme: the green of the sports field, the red of the wooded area, and the promenade with its long blue bench. I The sports field has four striking spatial elements. Each has a functional nature: a lamp post, a ball-trap, a water-pool and a sun-awning. The large playing-surface covers 7,500 square metres, with the pitch located centrally in the middle of the facility. This introduces a surprising sense of space into a district that is densely built-up. A small wood of copper-beeches lines the green field towards the adjacent school buildings. Seven different types of trees have been planted; their various shapes and heights are intended to form a red tree mass, providing variegated shadow, reminiscent of an English park landscape. I The colour series is completed by a bench made from 7,000 blue glass bricks. It is 160 metres long and three metres wide and runs the length of the promenade. The promenade itself gives definition to the large space in the middle of the park. Yet it also acts as an interface between the park and the outside, serving as a catalyst for communication and social interaction within the district. The bench and the trees on the promenade provide an inner space where people can walk and talk, and where at night the blue seat appears as a shining monolith, a functional work of art, creating a gigantic body of light, and giving this meeting place an unmistakable character.

DIPOL Landscape Architects was founded by Andy Schönholzer and Massimo Fontana in 2001. They consider it important to use integral design processes and interdisciplinary work, so that multi-layered projects can be created, in which the question of the site, particularly its identity, provides the focal point. In this context they have worked on a number of projects with the architect/artist Christopher T. Hunziker.

above:
Awning
mid:
General view
below:
Grove of copper beech trees

Project Facts
Builder-owner: Green City of Zürich
Building Time: 2004–2005
Size: 1.3 ha

141

above:
Water basin
mid:
Ball net
below:
Awning with basin
right:
Site plan

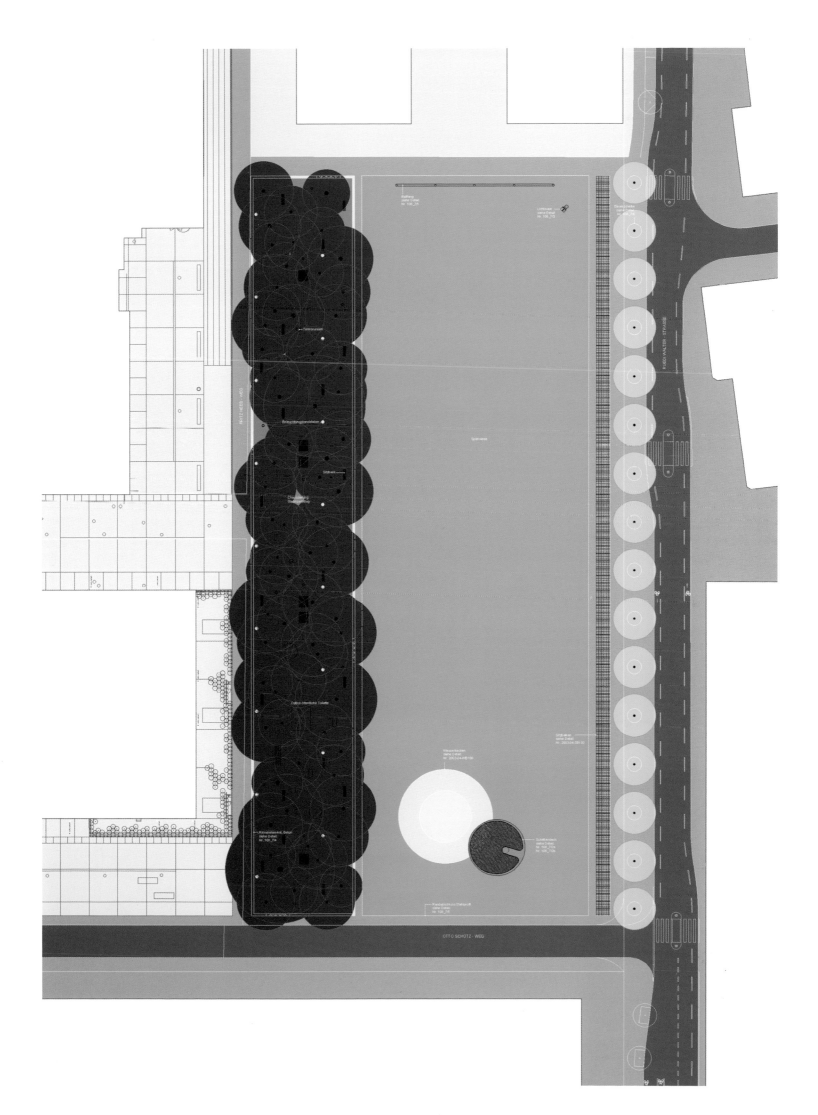

Rotzler Krebs Partners

This planning practice headed by Stefan Rotzler and Matthias Krebs, has been in existence since 1990. They work on the basis of a radical perception of what is there. They decode situations and problems and develop succinct images from them, which contain a provocative element through their uncompromising and unusual combination of things and themes. This releases energy in in viewers; creates aggression, joy, exitement, laughter.

Municipal Gardens Dornbirn

Dornbirn

In Dornbirn an old industrial site very close to the town center has been transformed into a municipal garden. Two factors shaped the design – on the one hand, the geometry of water-power and, on the other, the town's industrial history. The park layout is determined by the path of the subterranean canal, while a water-wheel, canal windows and echo-pipes bring it to life, providing a sensual and visual experience. The course of the canal likewise has a bearing on the layout of trees, pathways and linear elements, as well as influencing the way the parkland is divided into fields. I In the entrance area to the Natural History Museum, established in 19th century factory buildings, a particular collection of woods has been established. Trees are arranged on an imaginary map of the world according to their country of origin. I The central courtyard space inside the grounds has been designed as an urban square for general use. Its gravel coating contains iron ore, while a drinking fountain made from crude steel and a group of maple trees with rust-coloured foliage use colour and materials to emphasise the location's industrial heritage. I The former villa garden conjures up all the enchantment of a fairy-tale. Like the garden of Sleeping Beauty, it is surrounded by box hedges and white flowering shrub roses, while paths wind their way in between different conifers and venerable old trees. Anchor-shaped willow hedges create the spatial differentiation for a play-landscape, forming play-islands, each with its own particular composition. The water-garden likewise has a distinct shape. Planted with water lilies and reeds, it combines with the climbing plants entwined around the pergola to create a place that has a special poetic atmosphere and induces pleasant reflection.

above:
Sleeping Beauty's garden with
echo pipes
below:
Arboretum

Project Facts
Builder-owner: Office of the City of Dornbirn
Building Time: 2002–2003
Size: 2.35 ha
Architects: Dietrich | Untertrifaller Architects, Kaufmann-Lenz

above left:
Play area
above right:
Fence along the park edge
below:
Ground plan

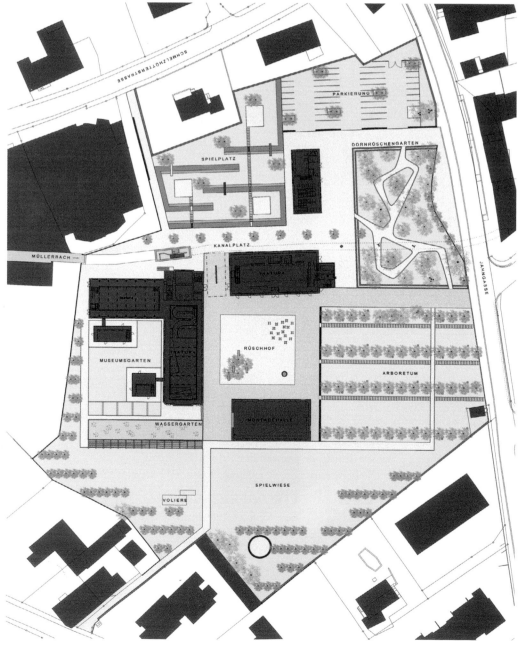

above left:
Echo pipes
above right:
Museum garden
below:
Water garden

Karin Standler

A graduate landscape architect with a PhD, Karin Stadler focuses on the quality of stopping points, representation and aesthetics. A central aspect of her work is open-space planning in the interests of young people for local authorities. The participation model developed by her practice, entitled "teens_open_ space", enables teenagers to join in designing open-space furniture at places which are important to them and to set up together in building workshops.

Andreas-Hofer-Park

Linz

The Andreas Hofer Park lies in a heavily built-up, central district of Linz. Conflicts between users of the park facilities – various age groups with different cultural backgrounds – were the occasion for redesigning the park, which had originally been laid out in the end of the 19th century, and for giving it a new and clearer zoning. The planning authorities reacted to potential conflicts of interest and a tight budget with a design which uses styling to define focal points of design. I To begin with, all shrubs were removed, to strengthen the stock of trees which had been inherited, and to give the park a permeable, airy and bright character. The trees, up to eighty years old, form the essential characteristic feature of the park, serving both as providers of shade and of spatial structure; they demarcate different sections – playground, recreational spaces and seating areas, young people's section, pedestrian paths, exercise area and green zone. The network of paths was redesigned and now links the park with its inner-city environment. I The central element is a hill, which functions as a separation between the different facilities, marking out spatial relationships. The hill and the depression form the essential structure of the park. The play area is bounded on the one hand by the hill, while on the other a bench sets a limit to the play area, which is at one and the same time a boundary and barrier to the street. A flying roof of concrete provides a seating area protected against the weather. I It was decided to have no flowerbeds, since it was the planners' intention that the park should produce its effect through its structure, not through isolated components of a "nice" kind. The materials used – few in number – point to a clear design principle, making the park both modern and functional.

above:
Southern atmosphere through
water-bonded gravel cover
below:
Play hill

Project Facts
Builder-owner: Municipal Gardens Linz
Building Time: 2004
Size: 3,600 m²
Further Participants: Karl-Heinz Klopf,
Gregor Mader, Rahm Architects

above left:
Recreation space beneath trees
above right:
Open space for young people

below left:
Small children's playground
below right:
Overall view

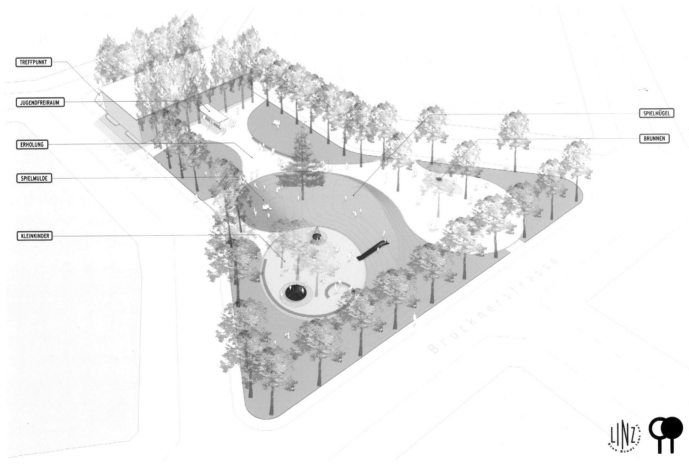

TREFFPUNKT

JUGENDFREIRAUM

SPIELHÜGEL

ERHOLUNG

BRUNNEN

SPIELMULDE

KLEINKINDER

LINZ

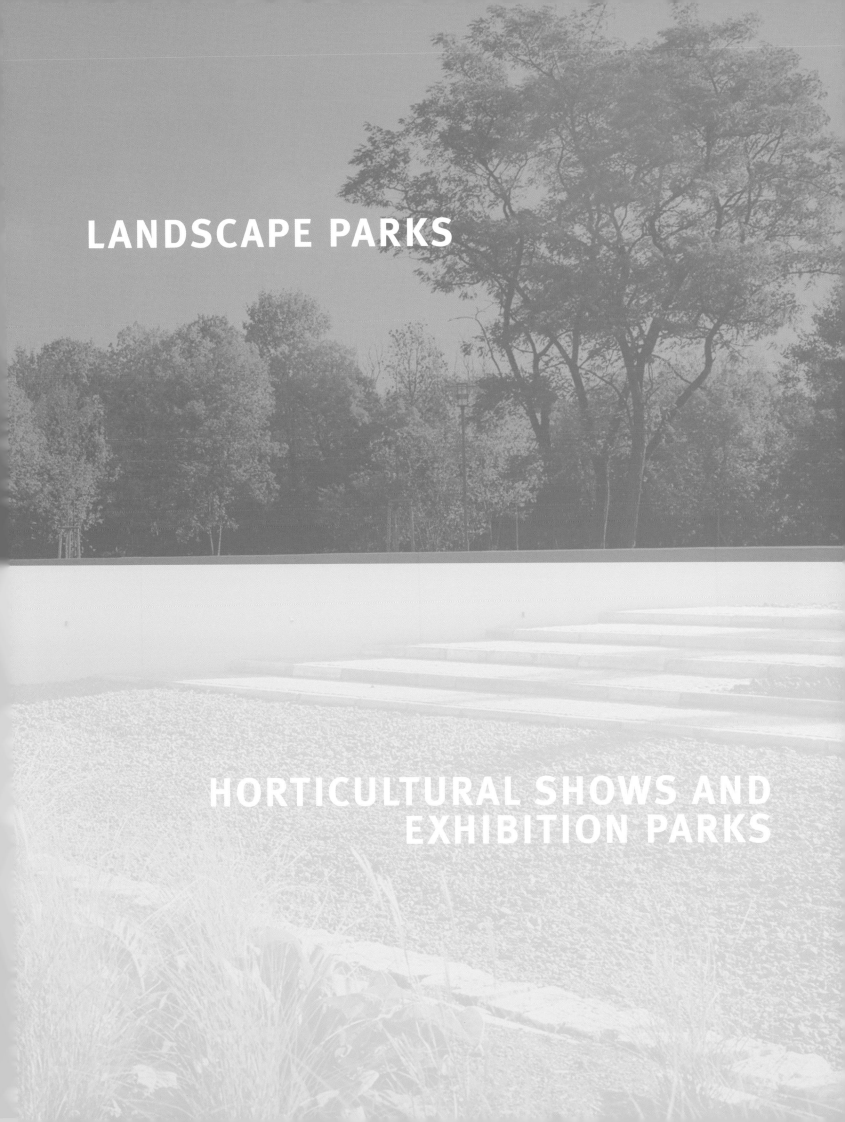

LANDSCAPE PARKS

HORTICULTURAL SHOWS AND
EXHIBITION PARKS

Schweingruber Zulauf

The firm dates back to the foundation of the practice in 1961; since 2005 this countryside-management practice has traded as Schweingruber Zulauf. Its heads are Lucas Schweingruber (*1964) and Rainer Zulauf (*1953). Both are graduates of Rapperswil University, where they are also lecturers. They are specialists in garden architecture and garden-monument conservation.

Museum and Park Kalkriese

Osnabrück

The museum park is located on the site of the Battle of Teutoburger Wald, a bloody encounter in which Germanic tribes slaughtered three Roman legions. In addition to the documentation of historical events in a new museum and annexes in the park (design: Annette Gigon and Mike Guyer) it is now possible to walk in the footsteps of history. A discreet monument was conceived in the form of a "landscape drawing", which is designed to catch the imagination of viewers. ❘ The former wooded location was afforested to approximate the surroundings where the rampart must have stood. A line of steel posts resembling a backbone winds through the landscape, marking in abstract fashion the course of the rampart. The posts are arranged more densely in the spots where there is certainty over the original contour, less densely where the route is the result of supposition – a design strategy allowing for adjustments based on new knowledge stemming from ongoing excavations. So it is that progress in archaeological research is rendered legible. ❘ An intricate network of narrow paths criss-crosses the wood behind the rampart and shows the manoeuvring room available to the Germanic warriors. 685 plates of Corten steel mark the Romans' defensive lines and their escape routes north of the rampart. The irregularity of their location evokes not only the panic and the discarded shields but also gravestones. At the "Time Island" an attempt has been made to reconstruct a section of landscape from the year 9 AD. A steel sheet wall frame provides a view over a wood of oak and beech trees standing at an excavated level approximating the geography of the time. In front of this area are sand banks and meadows with damp sink holes and ditches and between the two a section of rampart, newly erected as if by the old Teutons of yesteryear.

above:
The former battlefield
below:
The wall and the tower

Project Facts
Builder-owner: Varusschlacht im Osnabrücker Land,
Museum and Park Kalkriese
Building Time: 1999–2000
Size: 20 ha
Architects: Gigon Guyer, Zurich
Exhibition: Ruedi Baur,
Integral Lars Müller, Zurich

wbp Landscape Architects Engineers

Bagno Landscape Park

Burgsteinfurt

Outside the gates of Burgsteinfurt, in the Münsterland landscape park is the Steinfurter Bagno, a place with almost 250 years of history. The baroque park in the French style to the east of the Steinfurt palace, built in 1765 by Graf Karl von Bentheim-Steinfurt was important across Europe during its heyday. As a result of modifications and decay, in the last century the historic importance of the park could barely be seen. It was not until the extensive restoration of the concert gallery in 1994, which saved the last remaining building in the Bagno from certain ruin, that the foundation stone for the renovation of the entire park was laid. In 2002, with the participation by the town of Steinfurt in the "Regional 2004 – left and right of the river Ems", the unique chance for the landscape park to be restored arose. ▌The new development of the park draws on the historic basic structure. Its layers of time have been revealed by transforming them and making them visible again. The use of modern materials and elements – smooth concrete surfaces, yellowy-grey Dolomite sand and larch wood benches conforming strictly to form – underscore the contemporary design level. ▌Today the landscape park, with a newly designed entrance at the location of the former French Garden, which originally belonged to the count's family's private area, opens towards the town. Boulevards lead the visitor in and through the park to the Bagno square, to the former baroque axis with the concert gallery and on to the district of Borghorst. Newly freed lines of sight open up the dimensions of the landscape park and link the existing lake with its islands to the ensemble in the park.

Christine Wolf founded the practice in 1998; Rebekka Junge has been a partner since 2003. In their work they seek links and polarities between the inner and the outer, between buildings and open spaces, town and country, art and nature, form and ecology. Along with their work in planning and realisation, both are engaged in teaching and research, at Essen Combined University and Polytechnic, the University of Wuppertal, and elsewhere.

above:
The Grand Avenue
below:
The former French Garden,
the new entrance to the park

Project Facts
Builder-owner: City of Steinfurt
Building Time: 2003–2004
Size: 95 ha
Architects: Bebet Bondzio Liu, Münster (design),
Willebrand + Welp, Greven (construction documentation)

Latz + Partners

Duisburg-North Landscape Park

Duisburg

One of the most important projects of the International Emscher Park Building Exhibition was the Duisburg-North Country Park. Existing structures, designed for industrial use, were adopted, redeveloped and reinterpreted. Existing independent subprojects were given linkage – visually, functionally and conceptually; in their totality, they all form part of one huge land-art project, reflecting the hundred-year history of the region in a many-sided, impressive way. I "Bahnpark" (rail park), one of the sub-projects, was developed out of the region's historical transport routes. The lines of track form the most continuous linking components in the park. A large number of bridges provide original perspectives upon the various levels and the colourful vegetation, and ensure that the different sections all form a unity. I The area around the former sinter works has been converted into "Sinterpark": a flowering lawn and shady grove, framed on the side of the blast furnace by the remains of the crane track and a catwalk. It runs for 300 metres past the bunkers, providing a view down into the "Bunkergärten" (Bunker Gardens), which are built on various levels into the old bunker structures. I The Piazza Metallica in "Hochofenpark" (blast furnace park) is a symbol of the metamorphosis which has changed hard industrial buildings into a public space. Slabs which once covered the casting floor of the iron foundry now form the very heart of a green space. Eroded by natural processes from the very beginning, they will continue to rust and weather in their new location. I As you wander through the park, you will find play areas, inviting the walker every time to stop and play. In laying out these sections, particular attention has been paid to their contexts – both spatial and conceptual – thus emphasising, through adaptation and reinterpretation, the transformation of the old industrial area into a park.

The practice was founded in Aachen in 1968 and transferred to the Munich region 20 years later. The firm of Peter Latz, Anneliese Latz and Tilman Latz works all over Europe; its planning work covers urban-construction projects and urban design, large-scale landscape architecture, planning for open spaces, and ecological building. One major principle is: "The site and ecological programmes will build the spaces of the future."

above:
From the track walk the "Sinter Gardens" deep in the bunkers appear as pictures
mid:
"Walking where once trains ran" – the promenades of the Bahnpark
below:
Vegetation is taking over where once the ore deposits of the bunkers used to be

Project Facts
Builder-owner: Landesentwicklungsgesellschaft North Rhine-Westphalia (LEG NRW) as trustee of the City of Duisburg, Emschergenossenschaft Essen, Kommunalverband Ruhrgebiet (KVR) Essen
Building Time: 1990–2002
Size: 230 ha
Further Participants: Latz-Riehl-Schulz, G. Lipkowsky

above left:
Paths on the former railway
embankments lead into the
park
above right:
A square of trees in the midst
of steel giants: the
"Cowperplatz"
below:
The landscape park in the
projection of its surroundings

Projektionen

Der Landschaftspark

Landschaftspark Duisburg Nord

Latz + Partner   02 / 1991

Die "Hochofenstadt"

168

above left:
Piazza Metallica in the
Hochofenpark
above right:
Beech-hortensia garden in the
Sinterpark
below:
The "Rail Harp", a piece of
land created over decades by
engineering art

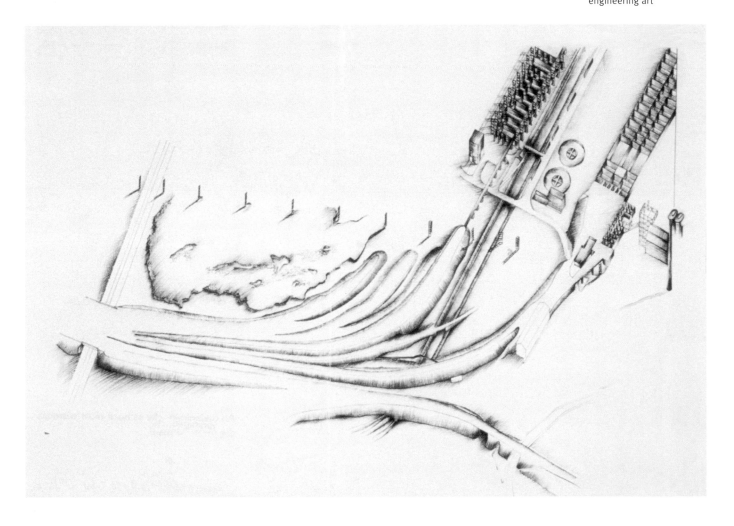

Working Group bgmr Landscape Architects and archiscape

Desert/Oasis Welzow

Welzow | The mining area of Welzow-Süd between Spremberg and Welzow in eastern Germany (Brandenburg) – unlike other locations – is expected to remain active until approximately 2030 and possibly longer. Under the title Desert/Oasis Welzow, the signs of mining are to be permanently portrayed over an area of more than 1,000 hectares. This new landscape explodes the dimensions of a park or a land art project. I The size of the landscape, bizarre shapes, loneliness and dryness in the mining area recall the myth of the desert. These images are recalled in the design. The creation of the new post-mining landscape spatially and temporally corresponds to the active mining. A band of the landscape, approximately 750 metres wide and 7,000 metres long, is being developed at the same time as the adjacent, active mine. I This gradual development increases the variety of the landscape as it creates a direct meeting of different „ages" of the landscape: Areas where the first vegetation has started to develop again border freshly tipped, desert-like areas. It is not the finished picture but just the changeability of the landscape which represents its quality. I The "Oasis" forms a counterpoint to the bare, surrounding landscape. Its hybrid structure shows basically landscape features, making it possible to incorporate different infrastructural uses at different times. Part of the design is to facilitate successive in-filling with buildings, without making this a definite principle. I With this project there is perhaps a unique opportunity to transfer the signs of the industrial process to a new landscape aesthetic. A landscape can be created which not only reveals the story of its use in the past but which also makes itself perceivable in space and as space.

The practice takes a particular approach to landscape architecture – it thinks of space and environment at various dimensional levels. A focal point of its work has been the design of broad-scale transformation processes in town and country. This has included post-industrial mining landscapes, as well as landscapes of urban culture on the periphery of cities. Landscape and city planning are mutually related in a reciprocal process.

The practice, founded in 1997, works at the interface between urban design, architecture and landscape architecture. At the center where these different disciplines overlap, an integrated and interdisciplinary approach has been developed to create new thought and expand boundaries. This mentality of symbiosis and synthesis encourages complex and innovative solutions in its application.

above:
Oasis, main building, and mammoth grove
mid:
Areas of waste tips from mining work
below:
Thematic design in area of open-cast mining work

Project Facts
Builder-owner: IBA Fürst-Pückler-Land, Vattenfall Europe Mining AG
Building Time: 2006–2030
Size: 1,200 ha

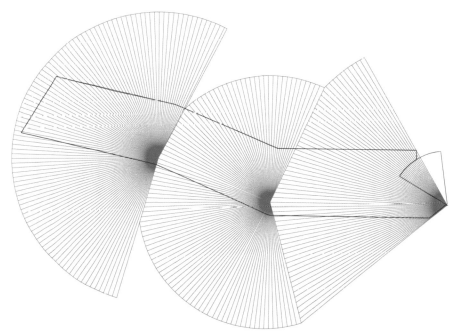

GTL Gnüchtel Triebswetter Landscape Architects

Conversion Maurice Rose Airfield

Frankfurt / Main

The site of the old airport Niddawiesen lies in the former flood plain of the river Nidda. It is protected as part of a conservation area of natural beauty and as part of the "Green Belt". The airfield Bonames was expanded in 1948/1950 by the US forces to include an asphalt airport with a tower and other buildings, mainly for helicopters. In 1992 the Americans left the site and since then large parts of it have been left to fallow. New user groups discovered the large space free of traffic for themselves and it is used for activities such as roller-skating, biking, inline skating, etc. I In view of the planning and construction measures, there was vehement engagement by the nature protection board and nature protection council to demolish and unseal the containment in the landscape. 3 of 4.5 ha total space was unsealed, 50 per cent of the asphalt was removed. The remaining 1.5 ha was defined as play and movement space. Except for two, the existing buildings were not demolished. I The site was worked so carefully that the character of the military space remains protected through its unique structure and materiality and at the same time the process of returning it to nature can be seen. Earth fields, modelled broken concrete and successive observation fields have been created. All changes, such as new plants and animals – also types that may disappear again – are precisely mapped and documented by the Senckenberg Research Institute. Apart from one copse, no new planting was undertaken. Leisure activities are spatially steered without requiring explicit allocation of specific areas. I The rough charm of the new site gives a new outlook on the many new design possibilities of public green space. One example of how a unique landscape is created with limited care requirements and high user pressure.

Markus Gnüchtel (*1958) studied landscape planning at the GHK Kassel and in Paris. In 1998 he took part in the Triennale XVII in Milan, with "Journey to Tahiti." Michael Triebswetter (*1961) took his degree at the Technical University of Munich Weihenstephan in rural conservation. After working several years as project manager in WLES, a firm for landscape architecture, they set up their joint practice in 1991.

above:
The runway heading into the country
below:
The earth fields

Project Facts
Builder-owner: Green Spaces Office, City of Frankfurt / Main
Building Time: 2002–2004
Size: 4.5 ha

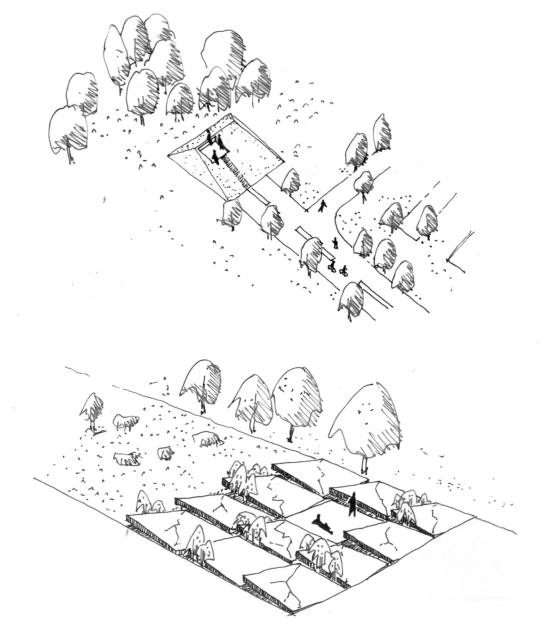

above left:
Re-using an airport in a
natural way, or natural
succession
above right:
From the runway to a popular
open-air stage
below:
Sketch plan of earth fields and
Belvedere

above left:
Seats made of gabions, filled with pieces of airfield concrete
above right:
The Nidda flood plains are coming into their own again
below:
Site plan

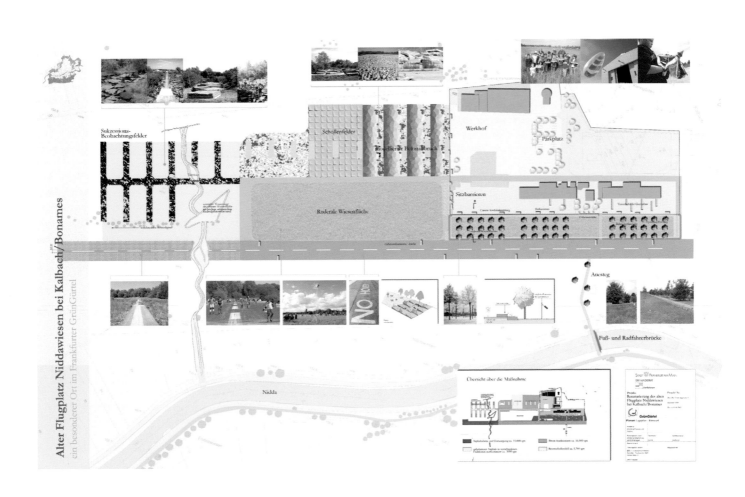

Gilles Vexlard + Laurence Vacherot – Latitude Nord Paysagistes

After studying in Nancy and Versailles, Gilles Vexlard (*1950) founded his firm in 1970, together with Laurence Vacherot. The firm undertakes various commissions, especially of an urban and suburban kind, from consultancy and part orders, right up to complete planning services covering every stage of work. Since 1985 Gilles Vexlard has also been a lecturer at the Ecole Nationale Supérieure de Paysage (E.N.S.P.).

Riem Landscape Park

Munich

South of the fair & exhibition center developing on the site of the former airport Riem lies this new park. The first planning stage was realised in collaboration with Stahr & Haberland, the second with LUZ Landscape Architects. I The design was essentially based on the location of the park, lying as it does between the wooded areas of Trudering in the south-east and the unwooded, man-made landscape to the north-east of Munich. With this as a starting point, two natural components of a typical kind provide the park with a kind of overall framework: light oak and pine woods, and spacious grassy heathland. The great forest ridges – the result of historical field layouts and the ecologically important wind direction – are placed in a diagonal, forming a powerful spatial framework. They are supplemented by smaller wooded structures, placed in a modular fashion. These wooded structures alternate with bio-diverse grassland, typical of the gravel plane. I Just like a municipal park, it features recreational facilities for the surrounding housing developments. The park is open to its surroundings and has a reciprocal relationship with them. It stands as a mediator between the city districts and towards the neighbouring man-made landscape to the east – a "Park without Boundaries", reflecting the ideas of Gilles Vexlard. Clear zoning – heavily-used sections, featuring a so-called activities strip, to the south of the housing areas, the bathing lake and the sledding runs, versus a landscaped section in the south – will enable the park to function successfully long-term, despite the wide range of uses required of it. I The activities strip has been particularly successful, being easy to reach from the residential areas, but so deep – 160 metres down – that it can cope with potentially conflicting uses. The southern section of the park has been left largely in its natural state.

above:
Seats in a lime tree grove
below:
The lake

Project Facts
Builder-owner: State Capital of Munich, represented by MRG Massnahmeträger Munich-Riem GmbH
Building Time: 1997–2005
Size: 200 ha

above left:
Groups of trees stress the
spacious meadow
above right:
View of the acivities strip
below:
Model

above left:
Groups of trees, arranged
symmetrically
above right:
Bird's-eye-view
below:
Site plan

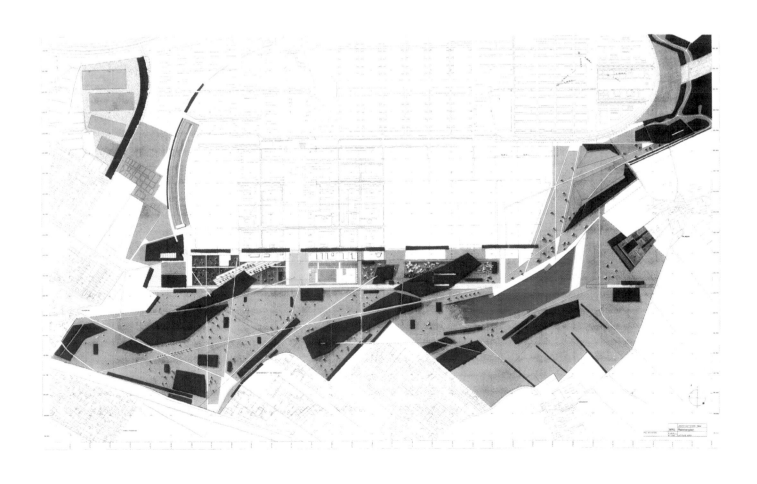

Atelier LOIDL

Projects realised by Atelier LOIDL cover a wide range in all dimensions – from villa gardens, to designing the outside grounds for an entire city district. The founder of the firm, Hans J. Loidl (*1944) relocated his center of work from Vienna to Berlin, not just as a planner, but also as Professor of Landscape Architecture (teaching project planning and design) at the Technical University of Berlin.

Hachinger Tal Landscape Park

Unterhaching

On the abandoned site of Neubiberg-Unterhaching Airport, covering more than 100 hectares, a park of regional significance is being constructed in a number of stages, featuring leisure and recreational facilities. An initial stage has already been completed. I The theme of the new Hachinger Tal landscape park is a playful approach towards dimensions, skylines and open spaces. The grand scale of the airport site has been preserved and developed further. The gigantic area of the runway is a fundamental element in the open character of the park. Mounds of earth create new skylines. Existing buildings partly disappear behind the new horizon. I To the west, the restored Hachinger Brook, and a newly planted near-natural alluvial forest, form an incisive edge to the park. Trees and shrubs form a green buffer towards the adjoining street. On both sides of the brook stone steps, wooden bridges and a water playground lead to the watercourses, thus making them easier to experience. The wet-dry zones and border areas are protected by limitation of access to selected support points. I For decades the airport site was closed to the public. Many species of plants and animals which had been displaced from elsewhere found their natural living space here. 250 species of plants alone, 31 bird and 19 butterfly species can be found here, including threatened species such as the field lark and the red-backed shrike. For this reason the large meadows have not been mown or pastured on any particular plan; the intention, in the long term, is to create an untouched grassland even richer in species.

above:
Detail
mid:
New horizons
below:
In the riverside forest when
still new

Project Facts
Builder-owner: Municipality of Unterhaching
Building Time: 2003–2004
Size: 35 ha

above left:
Locations in the meadow
above right:
Wild grassland view
below:
Western section of the park

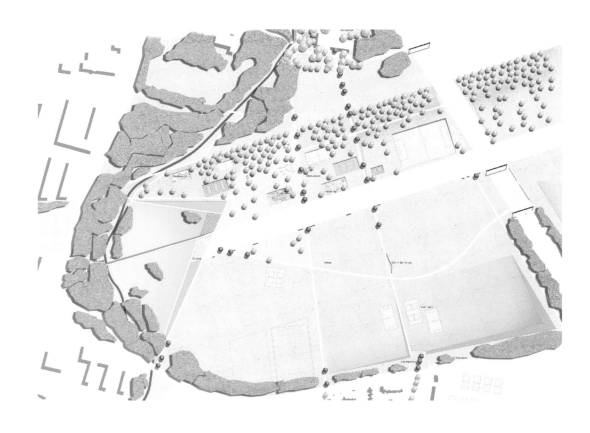

above left:
Shortcuts
above right:
"Restored to nature"
below:
Overall design

Auböck + Kárász Landscape Architects and Architects

Maria Auböck is a graduate architect
whose main focus is on urban planning.
After teaching at Rhode Island School of
Design, at the TU Vienna and at the
University of Applied Arts in Vienna, since
1999 she has been Professor at the
Academy of Fine Arts in Munich. János
Kárász studied architecture and social
sciences in Vienna. After that he taught
at several Universities in Vienna,
Budapest and Munich.

Blumau Landscape Park

Blumau   Because of the thermal baths designed by Friedens-
reich Hundertwasser, Blumau had developed into a
busy attraction to visitors, which needed to react
quickly to the streams of tourists. The task was to
develop a new landscape design, linking the thermal
baths with the village, which would attract the visitors
to the site, but which would also be accepted by the
local inhabitants. I The Safenbach forms the backbone
of the landscape park, situated on the western side of
the water. A main pedestrian path leads along the narrow stream, and to the east of this a spatial design was
developed, featuring seven "dancing tree lines", planted at staggered intervals, which follow the division of
the meadows and create an easily-penetrable com-
partmentation for the area. This basic framework –
supplemented by fruit groves – forms an intimate element of the design, redolent of history and tradition. I
Into this are inserted park-like segments: stand-alone
plantations of exotic woods, such as ginkgo, sweet-
gum and southern cypress; a groundwater pond,
planted in its flat-water zones with latifolia, yellow iris
and yellow marsh marigolds, with yellow pond-lilies as
an additional highlight; an inlet on the Safe, strikingly
distinguished by its stone configurations; and a sunken garden, featuring dry-stone walls, with sage, coneflowers, common mullein, catmint, bloodwort, day-
lillies and winter jasmine. A further layer is formed by
designs which reflect field crops, familiar from farming,
in an alienated form: vine trellises raised on split aca-
cia trunks, used as space dividers in the park, or sow-
ings of rape, sunflowers and purple loosestrife, used to
form areas of wild perennials. I Two wooden bridges
over the stream complete the design, while providing
the conditions for future development in the southern
area adjoining and a link with the accommodation
facilities which are being erected there.

above:
Pond
mid:
Surroundings of the pond
below:
Sunken garden

Project Facts
Builder-owner: Municipality of Blumau,
Provincial Government of Styria
Building Time: 1999–2001
Size: 13 ha

above left:
Dry-stone walls
above right:
Sunken garden
below:
Sunken garden – sketch of
plantation and range of
furniture

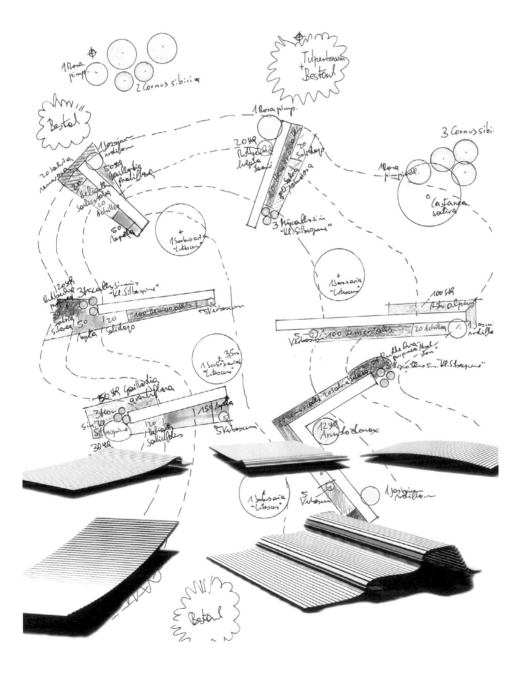

above left:
Wooden bridge
above right:
Double bench
below:
Site plan

Parkplatz Therme

Dorf Blumau

Wald

Therme

TOPOTEK 1

Martin Rein-Cano founded the TOPOTEK 1
practice in 1996; Lorenz Dexler has been
his practice partner since 1999. Starting
from a critical understanding of existing
realities, the search for design-approach
concepts finds its expression in clear
statements within the urban context.
TOPTEK 1 draws up proposals for independent projects, the design of which
reflects the needs of our times for varia-
bility, communication and sensuousness.

Post-Industrial Park,
Eberswalde State Horticultural Show 2002

Eberswalde

A former industrial area from the early 19th century
on the Finow canal, a historic canal in Brandenburg,
has been restored and transformed into a landscape
park. The concept for this post-industrial landscape
park is not based on an industrial-romantic experience but on mapping of the land which provides orientation. I The park distinguishes between intensive
experience areas and spatial width and offers a variety of details from painted situations to urban
asphalt graphics. For example, today the industrial
history can be experienced by looking at the
"Montage-Eber", which is both a crane and a trade-
mark of the industrial tradition. I The generous space
is laid out as a post-industrial park by a system of
paths. 40 cm wide steel bands, mostly accompanied
by walkways, lie in large wheels over the entire site.
They cover the new park like a network of meridians
and parallel circles. The bands give the entire park its
atmosphere. They visually mark the landscape area
which the old industrial plant formed and reformed
throughout its history. The artefacts are not exhibited
in hierarchies or a series of rooms, but are connected
by a dynamic framework. I In the area of the garden
band the equipment is collected for entertainment
purposes – inspired by museum-like forms of presentation – understood as a continuation of the cabinets
from the 19th century. Square themed gardens, each
approximately 150 square metres form the central
element of the park. They are the "cabinets" of the
garden show, a few small worlds with different exhibitions. An object inserted into the park subject to
consciously, artificially blossoming, scented and con-
stant change. This creates a living architecture which
reveals constantly new relationships between the
gardens.

above:
Ramp leading to the crane hill
below:
Landscape with paths of
steel strips

Project Facts
Builder-owner: City of Eberswalde
Building Time: 2000–2002
Size: 17 ha

above left:
Site plan
above right:
Long bench along the canal

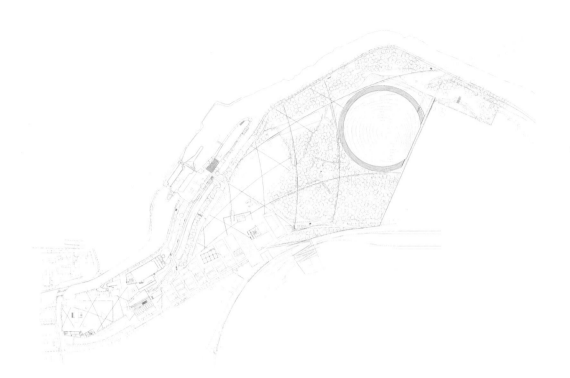

below left:
Themegardens
below right:
Lawn sculpture in the relaxing
garden

BÜRO KIEFER landscape architecture berlin

Wolfsburg State Horticultural Show 2004

Wolfsburg

The garden exhibition chose movement and the joy of discovery as its themes. The objective was to develop a type of landscape that embodies the force of kinetics and promotes physical movement in general. The theme of movement is expressed in the form of an earth model, a strip of minerals and a wooden jetty – a triple fringe extending around the edge of the artificial lake. I An island provides the chief feature in the overall design: not only does it function as a spatial determiner, it also accommodates the children's playground – the main attraction of the area. The informal atmosphere of the island sets it off from the other installations on the "mainland": it includes a range of play equipment, viewing platforms and large wicker structures. I A number of paths on different levels provide access to the gently rolling topography of the garden exhibition and lead visitors through a range of scenic backdrops. A continuous band of shrubs links the two parts of the horticultural show, the mansion and grounds in the northern section with the burgeoning modern park to the south. I Two separate principles inform the choice of trees planted on the Exhibition site – the flanking vegetation on the one hand and the foliage groups that give the area its spatial character on the other. Rows of Dawn redwoods bestow a striking form on the sculptural landscape and dense birch woods add their own special touch. The structural foliage is provided by stands of common and bog oaks, larch and willow. The grass cover is in the form of compact areas of monotype plants, with each species contributing through their differentiated vertical growths to the texture of the whole. The bushes and hedges, too are laid down along rigid lines and reflect the formal structure of the park landscape.

This practice, founded in 1989 by Gabriele G. Kiefer, is conceived on the idea that today open space is one of the last spheres with the potential for a "world counter-design." As a consequence, the design idea is built up on the concepts of clarity, reduction and a (transformed) reference to the existing environment – thus perceivable space as such becomes the main characteristic of the concept.

above:
During the State Garden Show outsize bank flowers set the scene by the lake, later to be used for water skiing
below:
The hill road runs through the modelled topography and the beech wood to the bastion

Project Facts
Builder-owner: City of Wolfsburg, represented by MSGA Marketing- und Servicegesellschaft Allerpark mbH
Building Time: 2002–2004
Size: 13 ha
Execution: nolte] hausdorf] sinai]: Free Landscape Architects

above left:
Observation bastion
above right:
Reed biotope;
Observation bastion

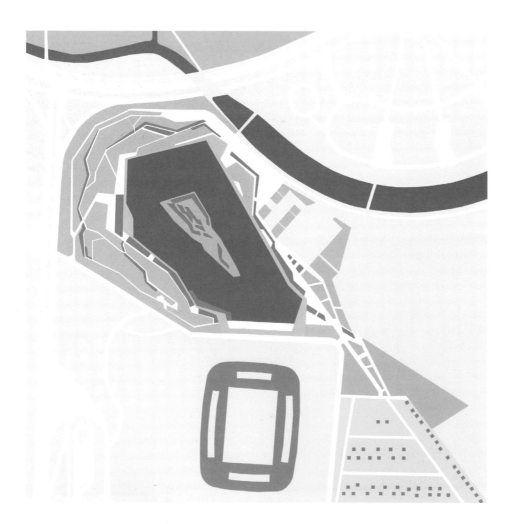

below left:
Site plan
below right:
At the lake;
Entrance area

hutterreimann + cejka

Wernigerode State Horticultural Show 2006

Wernigerode

The seven historical fish ponds on the edge of the town of Wernigerode in the northern Harz will provide the setting for the 2006 State Horticultural Show. Surrounded by industrial and farm land, blocks of prefabricated flats and allotments, the existing landscape had a disjointed quality, the ponds being spatially separated from each other. The project brings to the fore the location's hidden qualities, without erasing the vestiges of history. I A walkway running 1,000 metres from east to west – the "Fish Walk" – links the ponds. Along the walkway come the so-called "follies", designed as architectural features for walking along, planned by A-lab architektur, and providing a stage for water as an element. They serve to create a mood, to provide points of pleasure, drawing attention to themselves, attractions both during and after the Garden Show. The "follies" are various things – a waterfall for walking on, a translucent aquarium showing the various stages of fish breeding, or just large seats in the water. More than this, the "Fish Walk" is a "mineral mine", cutting deeply into the landfill, making it a geological nature trail, from the foothills of the Harz to its mountainous heights. Along the ponds, where there was once a dump for waste building materials, winds the "Garden strip", a series of 40 theme gardens. Look out for the "Recycling Gardens", in which building materials and demolition waste are turned into design elements. The gardens are bordered by the "Fenced Meadow" and also by the "Magic Wood." This is framed by a shining ribbon of perforated metal, and sparkling treasures on the woodland floor evoke the legend of the Wernigerode dwarfs. I The gently curving "Countryside Walk" provides a subtle counterpart to the brash linearity of the "Fish Walk." Thus a modern park has been created, displaying its own special regional featured in the balancing act between show and sustainable use.

On a decent basis of experience and pragmatism the practice works unusual, experimental and future orientated. From the concept to the architectual conversion their collaboration with planning partners and clients is based on economy, quality assurance and flexibility. She sees the quintessence of her work in an overlap between the new and the familiar, between reflection and imagistic poetry.

above:
"Fish Walk" with Folly
"water isle"
below:
Footbridge to the
"Zauberwald" (magic forest)

Project Facts
Builder-owner:
City of Wernigerode and
Landesgartenschau
Wernigerode 2006 GmbH
Building Time: 2004–2006
Size: 40 ha
Architects Follies:
A_lab architektur,
Jens Schmahl, Berlin

above left:
Egg yolk garden
above right:
Mineral gorge
mid left:
Colourful gardens

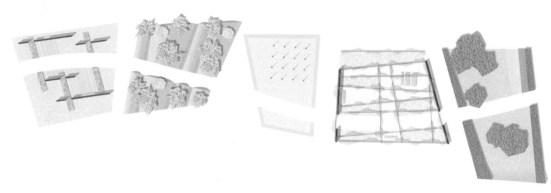

below left:
Competition plan
below right:
Grass patch

Landesgartenschau Wernigerode 2006
Ausstellungskonzept   M 1:1000

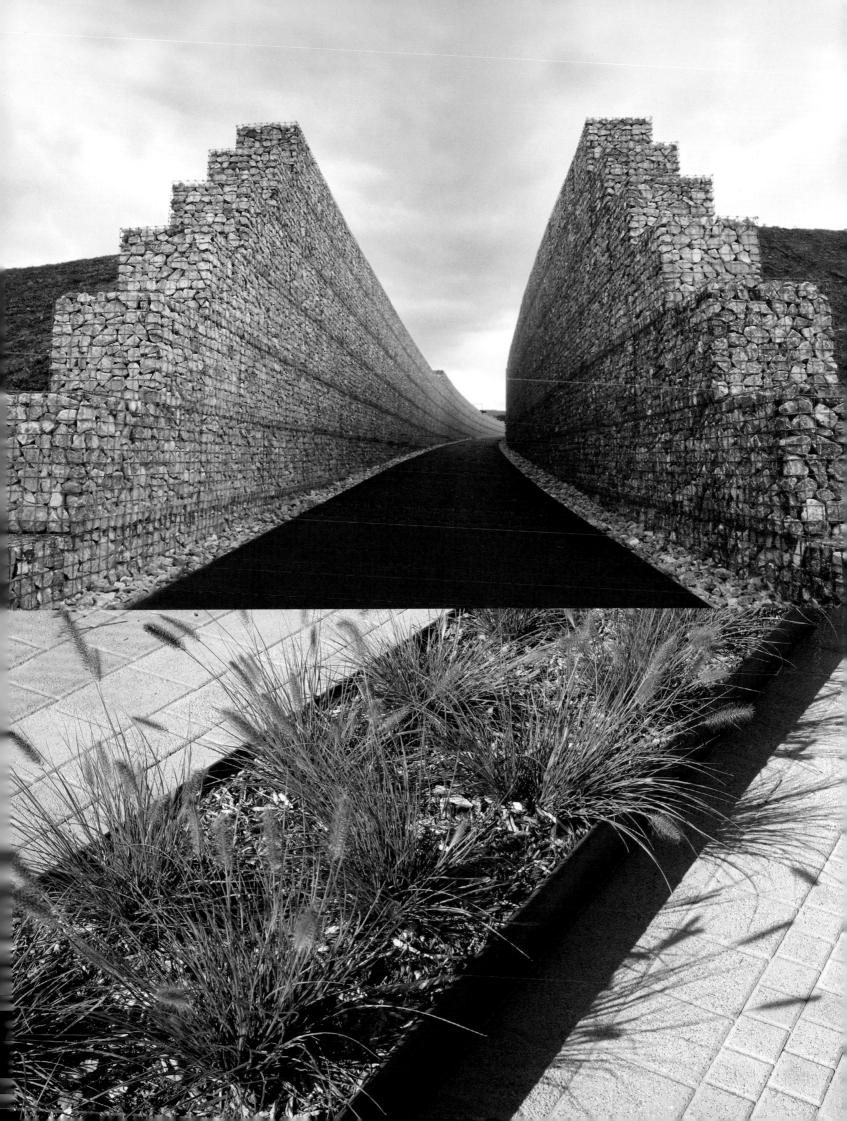

fagus with Dirk Seelemann Landscape-Architecture Practice

New Landscape Ronneburg

Ronneburg

Neue Landschaft Ronneburg is a part of the Gera and Ronneburg National Horticultural Exhibition for 2007; it is planned to make this exterior-design project into a permanent cultivated and experiential landscape. It includes the Gessental with the Badegraben and adjoining slopes. The terrain lies in an area of dramatic upheavals and changes to the landscape, for until 1990 uranium ore was mined here, using both open-cast and underground methods, and the resulting waste tips stretched right into he valley. Two completely contrary landscapes meet at this focal point: the cultivated landscape to the north, and the mining areas to the south, subject to turmoil over so many years. I In this context the themes for the design, that make this site unique, were developed. The existing disruptions, both in terms of the landscape and its history, were consciously elaborated. Thus the Lichtenberger Kanten, a massive landscape construction with a length of one kilometre, will bear witness to the scale of uranium mining on this spot. The building of the "Ronneburg Balcony" will provide a new urban edge to the valley, a new place for recreational enjoyment, with plenty of space for impressive vistas. I 12,000 ground-covering roses on the southern slopes of that Balcony will create an unforgettable experience of white, pink and red flowers, contrasted with the large number of flatly growing pastures. A further colour experience will be provided in autumn by the beech and oak groves which frame the festival meadow – "Indian summer" in Thuringia. I A "Grand Arboretum" is being built on one of the slopes: based on a strict grid of trees, theme gardens – so-called "microworlds" – will each show typical regional shrubs, bushes and flowers in a sophisticated garden design. Comprehensive sport and play facilities will supplement the plant and flower show.

The Dirk Seelemann landscape-architecture practice was founded in 1990; fagus, headed by Gabriele Seelemann, in 1992. Since that time the two practices have worked on a wide range of town-planning and landscape-architecture activities within the "green sector." The practice covers all aspects of garden and landscape architecture; the two practices give a slightly different weighting to their handling of these two areas.

above:
Experience the wide spaces of the Gessental anew
below:
A splendid show of roses on the terraces of the Ronneburger Balkon

Project Facts
Builder-owner: Bundesgartenschau Gera und Ronneburg 2007 GmbH
Building Time: 2002–2007
Size: 124 ha

above left:
Lichtenberger Kanten
above right:
Autumnal colours on the
Kirschberg
mid:
Play under the groves of the
Ronneburg Balcony
below:
In the Miniworlds in the
Arboretum

above:
View of the Ronnenburg
Balcony with discovery tower,
railway bridge and manor
below:
Site plan

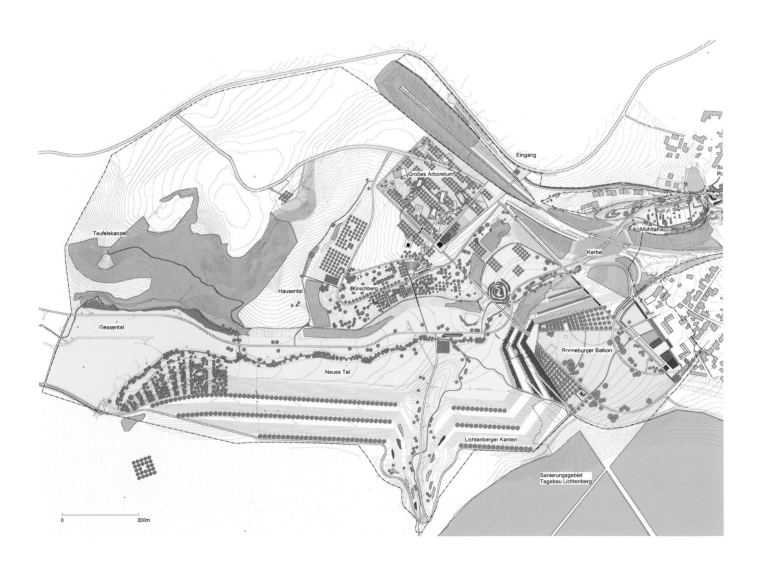

Schupp + Thiel

Lake-Park Lünen

Lünen   The Seepark Lünen at the 1996 State Horticultural
Show is a stepping-stone in the formation of the
Emscher Landscape Park, which was completed during
the development of the International Construction
Exhibition, carrying the same name. The main intention of the park's planning was to construct an environmentally and socially friendly relaxation landscape with liveable, useable space. In short: regaining the landscape. I The landscape space was scarred
by mining and its remains: pits up to 14 metres deep
and no functional or optical connections – plus the
remains of an ever-changing industrial landscape:
dams, pipes, canals, traffic links, banks of earth, old
storage areas, noise and smell pollution. I This natural park is a new type of residential district-related
relaxation space. The change from large and small,
open and closed spaces with integrated, function-
alised outside spaces such as play zones, allotments,
cemetery and sports areas characterises this park. A
special quality lies in the robust, multi-faceted structures, which can be used for various forms of relaxation and leisure, and in the direct allocation to the
surrounding residential areas. I The design theme
takes up the landscape's existing reference lines and
creates stable, new structures, recognisable signs for
orientation and a feeling of "home". The Seepark
Lünen is a public area, designed for the social and
cultural life of local citizens, a redesigned nature
space offering room for versatile social functionality.

The practice of Schupp + Thiel was
founded in 1991 by two landscape architects, Reiner Thiel and Professor Werner
Schupp. Since January 1999 the practice
has been continued by
Reiner Thiel as sole partner. In its work
the practice concentrates on project planning (public and privat outside installations, development concepts) and in
urban land-use planning (green-belt planning and expert environmental reports).

above:
The "Horstmarer Loch": grass
steps built into the slope in
front of the stage
below:
Beds of shrubs and pergola on
the promenade

Project Facts
Builder-owner: Landesgartenschau GmbH, City of Lünen
Building Time: 1993–1996
Size: 63 ha
Further Participants: Planungsgruppe Skribbe-Jansen GmbH, Münster

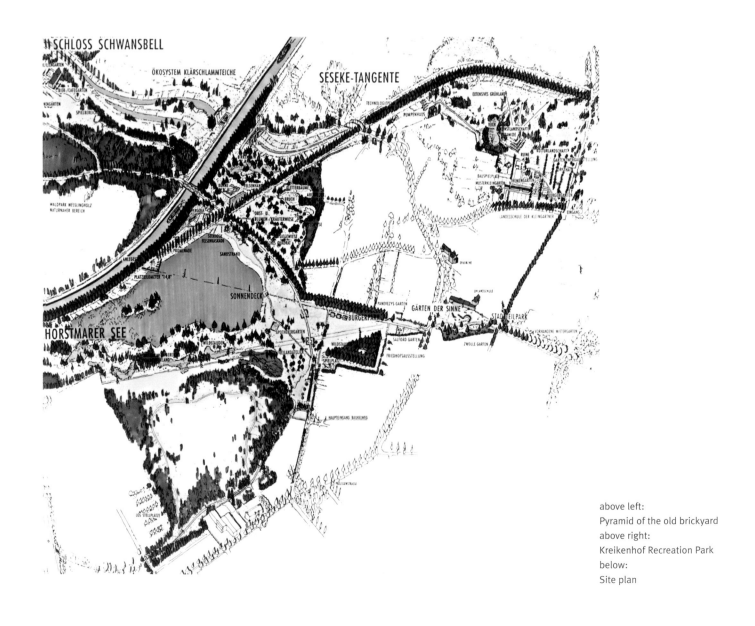

above left:
Pyramid of the old brickyard
above right:
Kreikenhof Recreation Park
below:
Site plan

above left:
Beach by the Horstmar Lake
above right:
Kreikenhof orchard
below:
Design for pergola on the
promenade

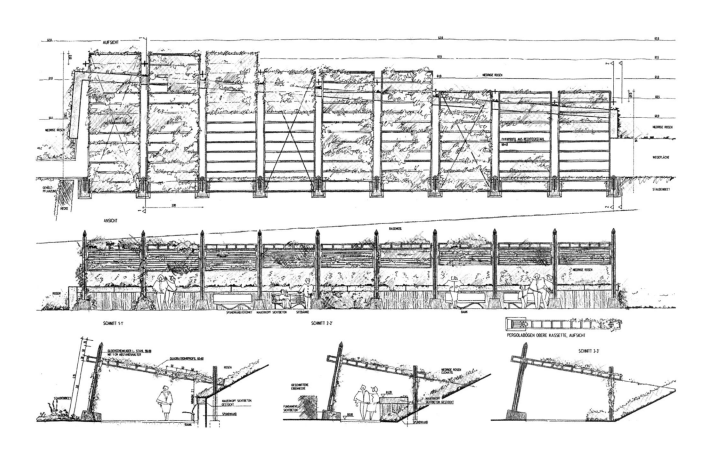

RMP Landscape Architects

New Gardens in the Dycker Field

Jüchen

For decades, the baroque Dyck water palace was the seat of princes and counts, now it is a "beacon project" of the 2nd Northrhine-Westfalia Regionale EUROGA 2002plus and is the heart of the State Garden Show which covers seven historic parks in the Central Rhine area. The beauty of the old park of the palace meets modern garden spaces in Chinese reeds. I Generously sized miscanthus areas, at right angles to a sweet chestnut boulevard, form the spatial structure of the former field. The historic boulevard is also the spine and backdrop of the new park. The miscanthus bodies correspond to the new lawns, which link the castle and Schlosspark with the Nikolauskloster and Dyck Wine House. Straight bands made from large-scale anthracite-coloured plates 1.50 metres across strengthen and steer the sight axes. The various garden spaces lie in the Chinese reeds, which over the course of their life grow to around 3 metres high. Over the year and as they grow higher, the miscanthus will "sink" into this sea of reeds. I 24 themed gardens with different possible uses and qualities form special islands, 14 of which have been realised by RMP. In the "White Garden" the preponderant features are white-blossoming shrubs, bushes, roses and spring and summer flowers. The uniform colour draws the plants together, reducing their effect on the whole. The psychological effects of the colour white – purity, neutrality and coolness – are underlined by the severe basic architectural structures formed by graduated tectonic plates. I A strictly graphic, linear plan characterises the "Plantwork Orange": the material of the bands and the structural steps is steel. The plants all bloom orange, together with blue-grey leafed undergrowth. Alongside the undergrowth, orange-coloured panes of plexiglass emphasise the vertical structure. The visitor follows the yellow-toned gravel paths between the steel elements.

The landscape-architectural practice RMP, established 1951, has been lead since 2003 by Stephan Lenzen (*1967). The model of a constructive landscape architecture leads to a non-contradictory form of open space, coherent in itself, so that all the elements engaged in the composition are fused into a homogeneous whole – you can add nothing to it and take nothing away; the result corresponds to the plan.

above:
Dycker Feld
below:
Orange plantation

Project Facts
Builder-owner: District Neuss,
Castle Dyck Foundation, Center for
Garden Art and Landscape Culture
Building Time: 2000–2002
Size: 32 ha
Architects: Schröder & Schevardo
Architects, Bonn

215

above left:
Meadow orangery in
China reeds
mid left:
Rückriem sculpture
on Dycker Feld
below left:
„Théatre d'architecture"
right:
Aerial photograph, detail of
„Plantwork Orange" and
„White Garden"

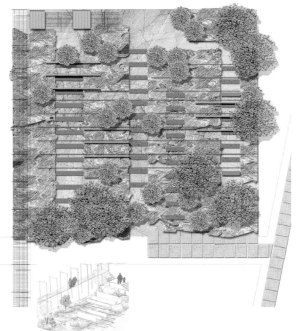

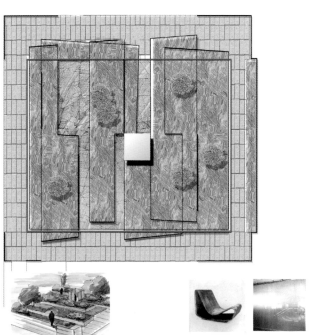

relais Landscape Architects

Projects managed by this practice, founded in 2001, range between an urban and
a landscape context, from city-planning
level to individual building. Gero Heck
(*1970) and Marianne Mommsen (*1972),
the firm's owners, regard themselves
explicitly as experts on landscape architecture, engaged in complex tasks in
close collaboration with architects, engineers and consultants.

Cargo Themed Garden –
Center for Garden Art Castle Dyck

Jüchen

The Cargo Themed Garden is one of 24 themed gardens in the Dycker Field, an area of the National Horticultural Show 2005 (overall planning RMP Landschaftsarchitekten, Bonn). In the opinion of the jury, the authors found the best response to the aims of the competition, showing both a sensitive and a modern use of plant material. The special quality of the design lies in the balanced proportions of the whole and in the successful handling of tension between the informality of the planting and the formality of the modules. I A wooden frame floats in a wide sea of Chinese reeds that marks out precisely a 25 by 25-metres area from the undulating grassy landscape. Nine wooden ribs structure the garden and bear a continuous band made from wooden boards: a pleasant area to linger, a sun deck for travellers in the garden. On one side, wooden boards have been piled up to form a generously proportioned bench. I From the outside, the static wooden frame changes with the seasons and vegetation periods into a stimulating interaction of the growth dynamics of the surrounding Chinese reeds and expresses this as exciting edges to the space. On the inside the wooden frame focuses on a 18 by 18 metres flowerbed. Two vegetation modules, alternating with beds of basalt and orchestrated by the wooden ribs, burst forth in a delightful spectacle of plant life. The vegetation modules are each defined by a pronounced image of flowers which grows from the use of matching types and sorts. Plants with different origins, exotic and domestic plants are gathered in this immediately effective vegetation to form stimulating neighbourhoods. I Specials are to be found next to the common. Cargo drifts between ease and formality, between agribusiness, allotment mentality and garden design.

above:
The dynamic growth of the plant life creates an exciting contrast with the severe wooden framework
below:
Wooden ribs give the garden its structure and carry a surrounding strip of wooden planks.

Project Facts
Builder-owner: Castle Dyck Foundation
Building Time: 2002
Size: 625 m²

above left:
The shelf of vegetation
emerges from the balanced
rhythm of the wooden ribs
above right:
On one side of the wooden
deck the planks are piled up
to form a seat
below left:
With all precision the wooden
framework stamps a 25 x 25 m
surface out of the rolling
grassland
below right:
The balanced nature of the
wooden structure

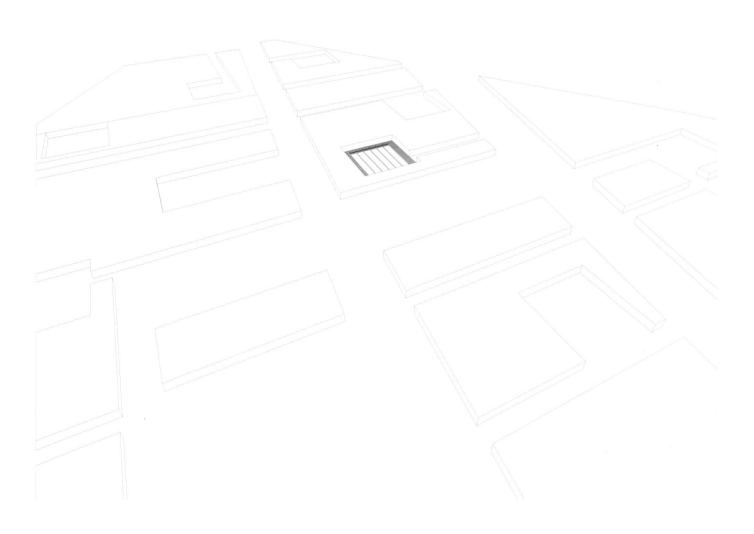

Wolfgang Färber Freiraumplanung

Wolfgang Färber studied graphic design
and landscape architecture and founded
his own practice in 1982. The aim of his
planning is to give some quality of life to
people in the most varied aspects of life. A
major aspect of this is a dialogue with the
four elements – earth, water, air + light –
producing the familiar, the surprising, the
exciting, the relaxing, and sometimes even
something totally new.

Kronach State Horticultural Show 2002

Kronach

In hosting the State Garden Show, Kronach had an excellent opportunity to take an area formerly under industrial use, with ground polluted by former waste, and to return it to its citizens as a local recreational area, while at the same time creating environmentally necessary retention zones for the Hasslach and Rodach rivers. The challenge of combining the needs of the local population and the requirements of water management was solved by superimposing park grounds, with a capacity for intensive use, and flood-overflow areas. I The 1.7 kilometre green swathe is divided into individual zones, clearly perceivable by their design, focusing on the theme of City – Park – Countryside. The area of the Municipal Gardens, with their dominant promenade of lime trees, ending in an urban terrace, and formally designed ground-floor areas, puts the spotlight on the urban scene. In the park spacious lawns offer the visitor facilities for recreation and games, forming a peaceful counterpoint to the colourful, strongly contrasted exhibition grounds on a flood-proof plane. I Flood-protection measures of various kinds were carried out – from the embankment wall to the water-collection areas in the green-covered slopes. A groin protects woody river-bank plants which have grown on the former flood barrage and which are now in the middle of the river, surrounded by water. Shortly before the State Horticultural Show was opened, these works underwent a severe test: the largest flood wave for 40 years swamped the grounds – and it transpired that all the planning was successful: the newly created retention areas were completely inundated, but the city was spared. Apart from a few "ground extensions", all the new installations – such as the paving, embankment walls and large trees – withstood the force of the water.

above:
City terrace and lime-tree
promenade to the city
mid:
A green area in the midst of
the central exhibition building
below:
View over the changing
flowers to the gabion ship

Project Facts
Builder-owner: Landesgartenschau Kronach 2002 GmbH
Building Time: 2000–2002
Size: 17.2 ha
Architects: Kochta Architects, Munich

above left:
Central exhibition area;
changing flowers;
Shrubs in the southern
meadow surfaces
below left:
Site plan;
changing flowers and foreland

above right:
Lime-tree promenade;
Adventure playground
below right:
Aerial photograph

OPEN SPACES:
WORKING AND PUBLIC LIFE

OPEN SPACES: LIVING

OPEN SPACES: RECREATION

OPEN SPACES: HEALTH

GHP Landscape Architects Gurr – Herbst – Partners

BTC Berliner Tor Center

Hamburg

The Berliner Tor Center lies in a borderland between dense, varied building developments and major roads. The building's structure divides the external section into street areas, courtyards, passages and border areas. Although the different areas are inter-linked, the overall space – due, among other things, to the unusual height of the buildings – cannot be conceived as a whole. I At the pedestrian level, the design focuses on the exterior, in a series of squares. These surfaces, with their light yellow concrete blocks, form a warm and peaceful basis. In contrast, the projecting areas formed by the ring of buildings, surrounding the former police headquarters, is paved in a dark anthracite. This "shadow" of the elevated buildings emphasises its plasticity and forms a barrier-free framework for the courtyard. I A passage, serving as a public thoroughfare, is marked by English oaks, standing in raised protection cages of corten steel. The southern section is dominated by a lively "sculpted hedge", consisting of five individual hedges, forming slanting planes. A row of white-trunk birches stands in contrast to this sculptural element, providing a particular emphasis, even in winter. The parking space at the existing building, forming the "Roter Platz" (red square), provides a particular emphasis to the overall concept. The red stone used here is supplemented with red-coloured leaves, to underline the particular characteristic of this location. I A high-top wood of 600 alders is developing into an expressive aggregation of trees, while their tops join to form a forest roof. This strong shape gives the location an unmistakable character, made all the fuller by the upturned beams of bright prefabricated concrete.

The objectives of the planning practice headed by Nikolaus Gurr and Guido Herbst are contemporary and use-related solutions. Variety is a must. Constructiveness and organisation are a matter of course. The range of projects covers every aspect of open-space planning.

above:
Elongated plant pot
below:
Forest of grey alders

Project Facts
Builder-owner: Dieter Becken, Investitions- + Vermögensverwaltung
Building Time: 2002–2004
Size: 1.2 ha and 1,500 m² roof greening
Architects: BRT Bothe-Richter-Teherani, Jan Störmer Architects

above left:
Elongated plant pot (detail)
above right:
The red square

below left:
Site plan
below right:
Forest; pollards

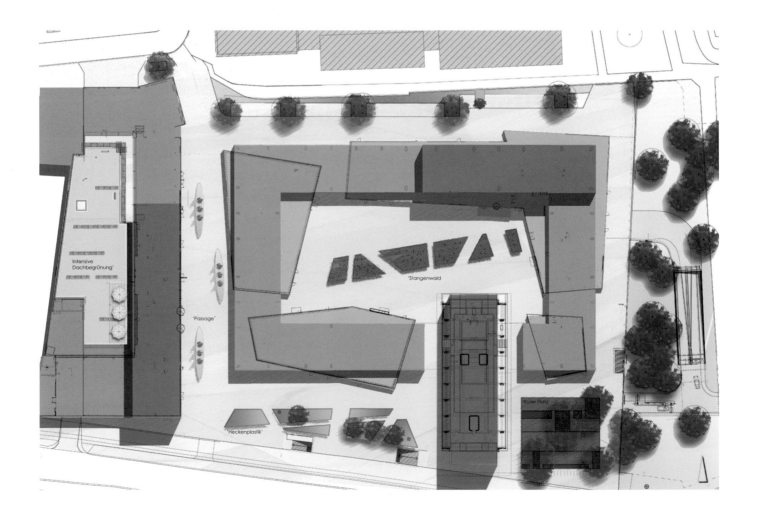

Krafft-Wehberg with WES & Partners

Grounds of the Representations of Brandenburg and Mecklenburg-Western Pomerania

The practice was founded in 1992; since 1998 it has had a planning collaboration with WES & Partners. Its philosophy is to bring out the potential of a site and its character, in the interests of meaningful and optimum realisation of required existing usage, and on this basis, after critical examination of city planning and architecture, to formulate strategies for solutions.

Berlin   The design concept for the grounds of the representations of two federal states in the so-called Ministerial Gardens takes elements and perspectives from the architecture and harmoniously develops them in the surrounding space. The building complex stands amid a landscape of lawns with pruned pine trees, reminiscent of the Brandenburg countryside. In the spring narcissi or blue-star transform the lawns into a carpet of colour. I Access to the buildings of gmp architects (von Gerkan, Marg and Partners) is via an incline. This compensates for the difference in height between the public path and the entrance, while steps made from blocks of natural stone lead down to the entry to the underground car park. The square is laid with slabs, likewise of natural stone, mirroring those in the hall of the foyer. It leads down via the foyer terrace into the garden. Terraces similarly extend the conference hall to the north and south into the open area. I The use of the same surfacing material on a continuous level, raised a step's height above the surrounding lawn area, creates a dynamic link between inside and outside. Spatial emphasis of this link is provided by concrete pillars, developed out of the architectural features of the walls. In line with the overall plan, the interior design of the ground floor is continued outside: two terraces made from wood decking lead down to gently sloping lawns. I The so-called Philosopher's Path along the west side of the property looks onto the garden and offers a haven of peace. This path joins the two terraces adjoining the conference halls and is bordered by hedge planting, punctuated by the occasional seating-alcoves.

above:
Salon terrace
below:
Site plan

Project Facts
Builder-owner:
States of Mecklenburg-Western Pomerania and Brandenburg
Building Time: 2001
Size: 1,920 m²

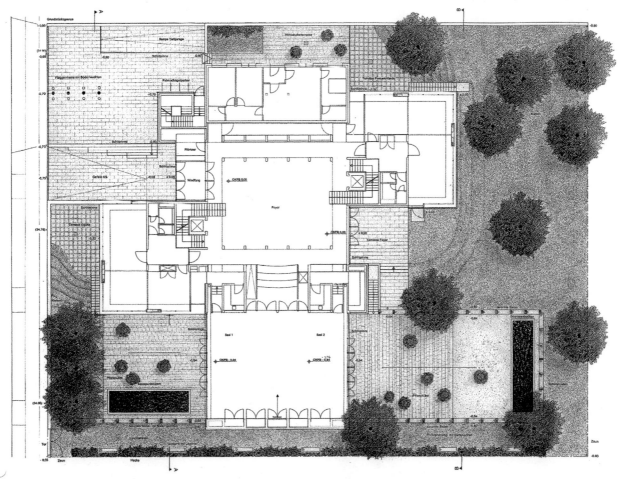

above left:
Wooden terrace to the
basement
above right:
Salon terrace to the west
below:
Interplay of ground and
facade

above left:
Lawn modelling towards the basement
above right:
Bamboos close the salon terrace to the east
below:
Terrace with view towards the garden of the State Representative Offices

B . A . E. R. Architects Landscape Architects Engineers

Center of Innovation for Environmental Technology, Outdoor Facilities

Stephan Becsei (*1957) and Christine Hackenbracht (*1955), both graduates of Kassel Combined Polytechnic and University, founded their own practice in 1989. It has the following philosophy: "To confront the site with integrated, resolute forms and clear concepts. Transience is beginning now – nature will claw everything back." Their work covers city squares, pedestrian zones, rainwater management, lighting concepts and lighting design.

Berlin　On the grounds of the former Academy of Sciences in the district of Adlershof the last few years have been spent developing the science and technology park WISTA. When it came to landscaping the open areas belonging to the Innovation Center for Environmental Technology, the design was based on predetermined spatial structures and the contextual references of the space-allocation plan. The interdisciplinary planning process involved the close collaboraton of the architects Eisele+Fritz, Bott (Hilka, Begemann). It ostensibly extends and enhances the design of the building through the medium of its external space. Particular aspects of the building design have likewise been influenced by elements of open-space planning. I The differential use of certain parts as paths and recreational areas provides the basis for the design. Depending on their function, they are made from concrete, natural stone, wood, steel, water and vegetation. I The main path is built using large prefabricated concrete units containing integral lighting. It provides the main link to the science city. Access to the 450 metre long building opposite is via the inner courtyard down diagonal, concrete-slab paths. These are set at the level of the floor of the building. The interplay of diagonal lines of various widths with the staggered paths lengthways leading to the rainwater reservoir gives the open space a right-angled structure. I The recreation areas are marked by limestone paving to provide a contrast in size and colour. They contain large concrete benches. The water basins serve a necessary purpose by capturing rain overflow. Yet, at the same time, their design adds to the relaxing quality of these areas. Every effort was made to preserve the stock of existing trees. Integration into the open-space planning reinforced their perceived importance. A floating concrete table under the shadow of the trees creates a raised recreation and storage area. It also provides a focus point for the rear of the open area towards the Nernststrasse.

above:
View from the inner courtyard to the diagonal path with the remaining trees
below:
View of the inner courtyard from the south

Project Facts
Builder-owner: WISTA Management GmbH
Building Time: 1996–1999
Size: 1.4 ha

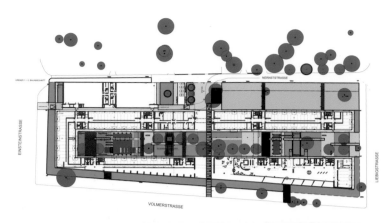

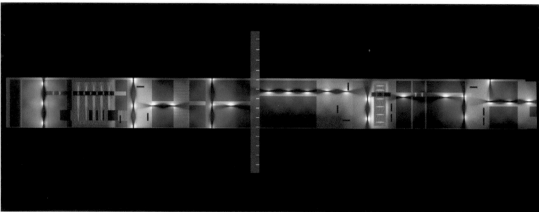

above left:
Site plan
above right:
Tank with walkway
mid left:
Lighting simulation in the
inner courtyard with the path
axes
below left:
Central axis through the
courtyard
below right:
Concrete strips in the lawn

Harms Wulf Landscape Architects

Hannah Arendt Grammar School

Berlin

The conception for the new high-school is the result of a competition from the early 90s for the new residential area Rudower Felder in the south of Berlin. Corresponding with urban development intentions, the school premises are diagonally crossed by a public path. The open space planning uses this fact and divides the space into a sports area in the north and a schoolyard in the south, with the visual connection being produced by a uniform grass area and the homogeneous planting of trees. The school site, on the main axis of the residential district, forms the southern closure of the site. I A uniform covering as connecting design element links the entrance area of the school to the ground floor section and the schoolyard. Play platforms, street ball baskets and a football area structure the large site and allow for the needs of the pupils. I A strip of hedge to one side allows outdoor lessons and borders the open spaces of the neighbouring sports hall. An essential and attractive part of the hedge-strip is a wetland towards which the run-off from the whole site is collected and drains. I An area at the end of the hedge opens up the sports fields in the north of the site. The spatial relationship to the sports hall is formed by a free-standing concrete wall. In contrast to the clear boundaries of the school playing fields, the sports hall's surroundings merge into the public paths through the district. A playground, with a coloured plastic covering, inclining towards the sports hall, has developed into a popular meeting place for youths, especially because of its topography.

This graduate rural conservationist has had his own practice since 1992. The practice aims at an ideal synthesis of existing circumstances, functional requirement and aesthetic qualities. It attaches great importance to the correspondence of the formal vocabulary of structural and landscape architecture. This applies to the design of backyards as well as parks, for the use by people of any age – with or without handicap.

above:
Wetland with walkway
mid:
Square with sports areas
below:
Seating steps, forecourt sport-shall

Project Facts
Builder-owner: District Office of Berlin-Neukölln
Building Time: 2000–2003
Size: 1.8 ha
Architects: Alten-Architects

above:
Hedge garden / school garden
below left:
Bicycle frame (office design)
below right:
Synthetic coating forecourt
right:
Site plan, design

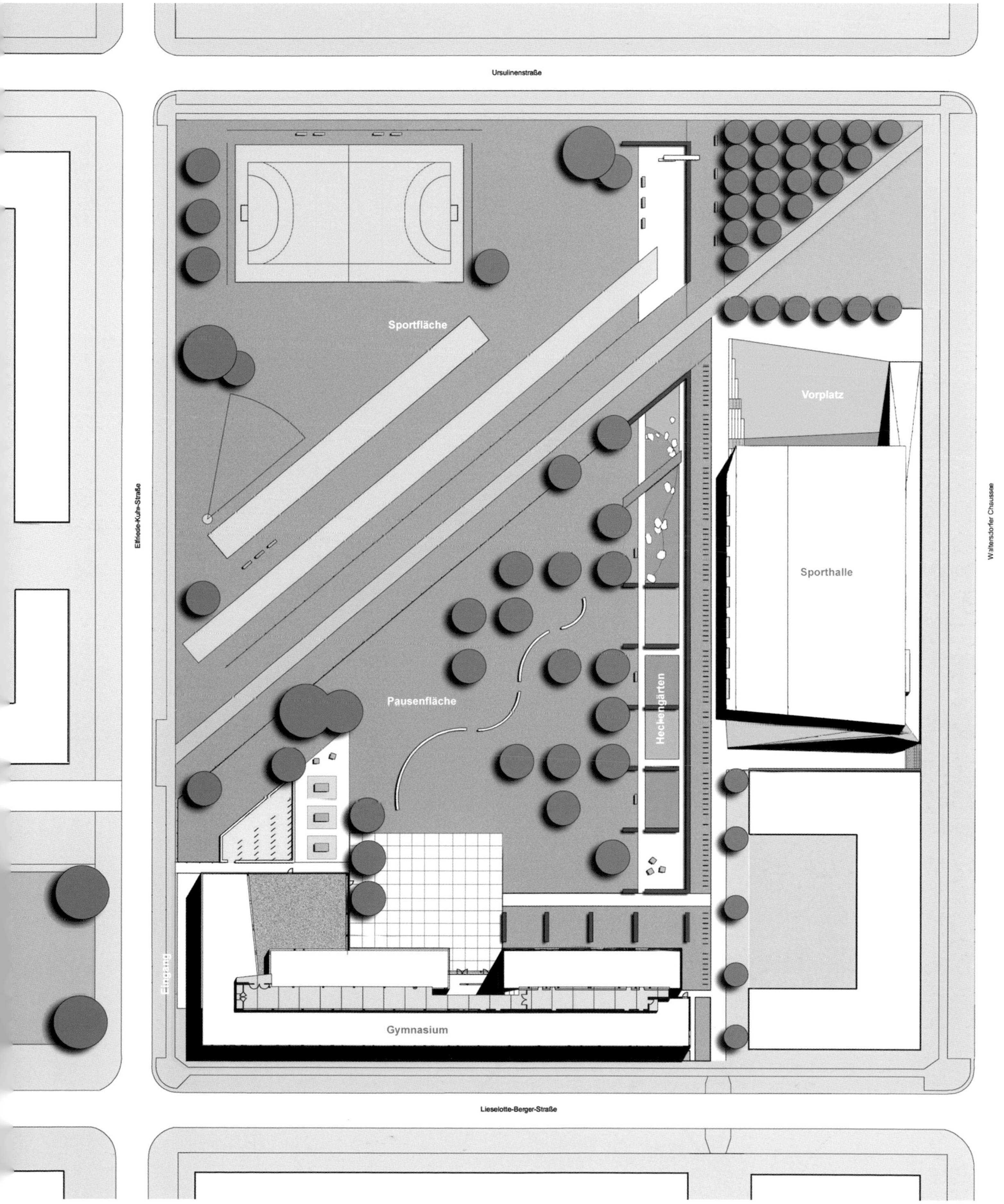

Ursulinenstraße
Sportfläche
Vorplatz
Elfriede-Kuhr-Straße
Sporthalle
Waltersdorfer Chaussee
Heckengärten
Pausenfläche
Eingang
Gymnasium
Lieselotte-Berger-Straße

Stötzer Neher Landscape Architects

VW – The Transparent Factory

Peter Neher is the owner of the practice, founded in 1973, which also has a branch in Berlin, run by Hans-Jörg Wöhrle. The aim is to develop, from an analytical and dialogue-based planning process, a form which defines the site in a simple and incisive way, and which will remain distinctive. The work of Stötzer und Neher connects architecture and landscape, art and nature as well as the people with the places.

Dresden   The Transparent Factory was not built in an industrial zone on the borders of Dresden, but in the very heart of the city, directly adjacent to the Grosser Garten. This production plant, designed from plans produced by Henn Architekten Ingenieure, made Volkswagen the first manufacturer to create a production concept linking the processes of traditional car production with manufacture work. **I** The Transparent Factory is a place of transparency and interchange, making the experience of car production visible to the outside world. The spatial facilities and combination of materials used in the building provide a new quality of customer service, aided and extended by the design of the environment. **I** Unusual forms of building which encourage curiosity have been incorporated into a multi-faceted landscape architecture. While the facades facing the street convey a closed, strictly logical impression, the open spaces, with their clear shapes, suggest an open liberality. On the side facing the Grosser Garten an architectural game of free-standing masses has been created; the outdoor areas are characterised by flowing contours and green spaces. **I** The exterior is designed as a garden, enclosed by a frame. Various natural theme zones within the garden present a contrast to the glass facade and the black, shining, representative entrance platform. Bridges link the frame with the entrance level, so that the building and its open space can be understood as a totality.

above:
Bridges provide
noticeable transitions
mid:
The components are
characterised by
function and form
below:
Architecture and countryside

Project Facts
Builder-owner: Volkswagen AG
Building Time: 2000–2001
Size: 6.2 ha
Architects: Henn Architects, Berlin

above left:
Nature and Technology;
View of the glass facade
above right:
Clear landscape forms
below:
Site plan open space
construction

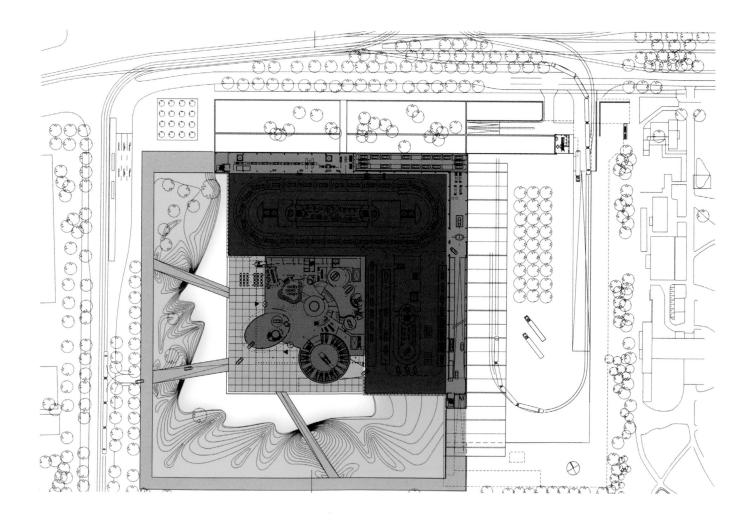

above left:
Entrance
above right:
VWs green surroundings in
Dresden
below:
Sketch

stock + partners

stock + partners was hived off in 1999
from the firm Stock + Ehrensberger. The
firm's founder, Wolfram Stock completed
his apprenticeship in the Botanical
Garden Cologne in 1979, after which he
studied landscape architecture and worked for the municipal garden department
in Erlangen. His partner in the practice is
Tim Hofmann who has a degree in garden
and landscape architecture. The practice
works in landscape and green-belt planning, open-space and garden design.

Open Spaces of the Medical Department, Friedrich Schiller University

Jena

The design of the open space of the new clinic is based on the aims of the Jena landscape plan from 1993. An existing greenbelt area from the Saale meadows through the Neu-Lobeda estate now reaches to the Drackendorfer Park. By interweaving the traffic flows, the central green space remains mostly traffic-free. Access for emergency vehicles and for deliveries and collections is from the north, access for patients, employees and visitors is from the south, which is also where the central car park is situated. Within the framework of the overall concept, the various areas of the new park area are planted individually to give them their own character. I The guiding principle is to lock in the building with the open landscape and to penetrate the geometrically designed green spaces around the building with a naturally arranged green area. The core of the open spaces is the plaza with trees and drinking fountain at the main entrance and the large pond with the tree island in the central green area. A second square with pond and tree area is positioned in front of the A+E entrance. Small, quadratic tree areas with various blossoming trees divide the area around the new clinic building. I Apart from asphalt areas, layered concrete walls and quadratic concrete plaster, only shell limestone, in various shapes, is used: as cut covering on the plaza, as blocks on the promenade, crushed blocks in the gabions of the rain water basins, gravel in the paths connecting the waterways and gravel in the car parks and on emergency access routes.

above:
Ground with trees
mid:
Small pool
below:
Emergency reception – ground
with trees

Project Facts
Builder-owner: Jenoptik MedProjekt GmbH
Building Time: 1999–2004
Size: 18 ha

above left:
Rainwater pond
above right:
Promenade
mid left:
Shrubbery
mid right:
Courtyard cafeteria
below left:
Miscanthus and verbena
below right:
Dry shrubs

above left:
Rainwater-overflow pond
above right:
Large pond
below:
Site plan

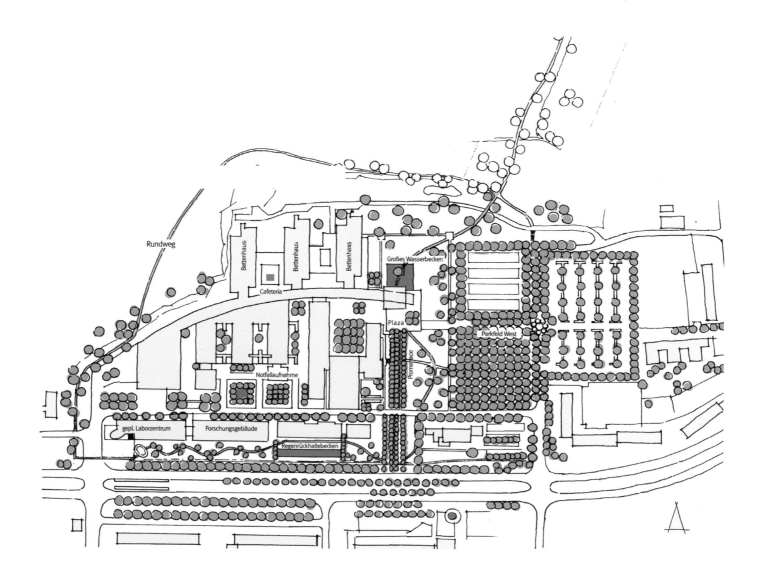

Rainer Schmidt Landscape Architects

The philosophy of the business, founded

in 1991, is to find answers to the prob-

lems of our times, aware that the land-

scape architecture of the twenty-first cen-

tury should be a realistic reflection of

how people come to terms with each

other and with nature. Rainer Schmidt

attempts to realise these answers in

designs, thus finding a balance between

design, functions and feelings.

Johann Gutenberg Grammar School

Erfurt

Following a schoolboy's shooting spree which ended with 16 people dead a new pedagogical concept had to be found for the Johann Gutenberg grammar school and the necessary rooms created that would enable pupils and teachers once more to derive some joy and satisfaction from interacting with one another. At the core of the design for the extension of the school building and the redesigning of the open-air areas was an unusual "pupils' platform" that is aligned with the axis of the building and provides a kind of democratic base for the majestic old school. ❙ This platform, which can also serve as a stage, starts at the publicly accessible square Gutenbergplatz and ascends to the school's main entrance alongside a sweeping open-air staircase. The steps promote communication and are a major feature of the newly designed square, which with its sparse trees retains an untrammelled view of the building. The platform continues through the foyer of the old building and into the rear schoolyard, passing through the assembly room and the sports halls. It is the prolongation of the public street through the building and gathers together the communal rooms of the school itself. ❙ In the rear of the building the pupils' platform forms the central axis of the schoolyard and is dotted with areas of grass and shrubs and with low walls designed as seating. On both sides the schoolyards drop away in tiers to the level of the sports hall. As a counterpoint to the two existing lime trees in the schoolyard a number of individual, multi-trunked flowering trees have been planted on the terraces. The individual levels, alternating between hard surfaces and plant and grass cover, reflect the uses to which they can be put. The entire schoolyard is also open to young people from the locality. The school platform is the venue for public events.

above:
The platform runs through the foyer of the old building into the schoolyard at the rear
below:
Terraced schoolyards with areas for activities and recreation

Project Facts
Builder-owner: State Capital of Erfurt, represented by Structural Engineering Office of the City of Erfurt
Building Time: 2003–2005
Size: 8000 m²
Architects: K+P Architects and Town Planners

above left:
The terraces provide a wide
range of spaces
above right:
The student platform as the
central axis of the schoolyard
is divided by seating walls and
planted area

below left:
General plan
below right:
The linear design is emphasised by the contrast between
the materials used

Pfrommer + Roeder Free Landscape Architects

Department of Computer Sciences

Stuttgart

This new building for the Department of Computer Sciences is part of a complex, consisting of institute buildings, students' refectory, and attractive grounds which date from the Seventies. An integral component in a so-called "learning highway", it is part of the center of university life. I The rooms in the Computer Sciences Building feature a transparency and openness which increases from the outside inwards. The particularly light construction of the supporting framework, and the use of daylight in all rooms and lecture halls, minimise the boundaries between the inner and the outer. The use of transparent, translucent and reflective materials creates a spatial perception hovering between illusion and reality. I The interior courtyards have been thoroughly incorporated into this system of complex visual relationships, not only to increase the building's transparency, but to create external areas which are set apart from the campus, serving as recreational, working and observation spaces, all in one. A single design motif – that of "living room" – runs through all four courtyards, allowing them to be distinguished one from another. Thoroughly integrated into the daily operation of the Department, and into its teaching, this theme was chosen as a counterpart to the high-tech world of the Department's work. I Various types of carpet were laid in the upper storeys – Berber, Persian, sisal and flokati – to make a platform to walk on. Their appropriate furnishings, and the play with the proportions of carpet, chairs, lamps, potted plants and people, create a slightly bizarre atmosphere. In particular, the outsize, bright yellow flower pots on the lower ground floors, which can be seen from the lecture halls, corridors and campus, seem to be from another world – confounded by their size, the onlooker has a chance to escape academic reality for a moment.

Dieter Pfrommer (*1954) studied at Wiesbaden Polytechnic; since 1978 he has been a freelancer, and since 1987 has also been working as an expert for landscape-architecture services and charges. Ulf Roeder (*1962) took degrees at Berlin Polytechnic, Nürtingen Polytechnic and Toronto, and since 1991 he has been working as a freelance landscape architect. One of the focal points of their work is the design of garden shows.

above:
Light-grey gravel for a grainy "berber"-effect
below:
Strips of artificial lawn for an accessible "Floccati"

Project Facts
Builder-owner: State of Baden-Wuerttemberg
Building Time: 2002–2003
Size: 1,800 m²
Architects: Building Authority of the Universities Stuttgart and Hohenheim
Further Participants: Hendrik Scholz (project management), GU Müller-Altvatter (construction documentation, contruction management)

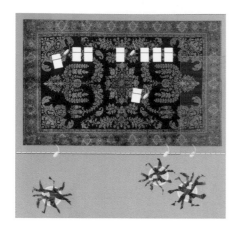

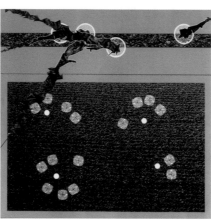

above left:
Drafts carpet typologies
above right:
Oversized plantpots connect
the different courts and levels

below left:
The floral ornaments reflects
the "classic" of carpets: the
Persian
below right:
Fine-structured oakwood
planks represent "Sisal"-
carpeting

Peter Kluska

Robert Bosch Foundation

Stuttgart

Along the construction of the new Heidehof Bosch Building by Peter Kulka, a new garden layout was merged with the park of the Robert Bosch Villa to form a spacious new open-air complex. I The design of the garden around the new building strongly reflects the principles of its architecture: the cubic shape of the new building, the spacious entrance square, and its openness to the countryside were all adopted into the plan for open spaces. Two groves of trees, related closely to the structure and featuring pruned plane trees, complement the space-creating complex of architecture and nature. Other aspects include clear cubes of pruned beech and a long stretch of stepped flower-beds. Broadening out to the north, the garden's modelled topography provides space for a sculpture by Bernar Venet. I A further path, designed as a circular walk, links the new garden with the roads in the park round the villa. From the entrance square, a broad staircase, let into the historical supporting wall, leads directly to the forecourt of the Robert Bosch House. Here, in the historical park, the spatial design is governed by the existing stock of trees that partly had been in existence when the villa was built in 1910. The marks of the garden's history – spatial structure, sight lines, relief designs– were used as the basis for all changes and planning. I The look-out terrace was restored, enlarged, and axially connected with the villa terrace. The water installation of the Römerbad (roman baths) was renewed, the lake restored and enlarged so that water motives are bringing new life to the park.

Peter Kluska, a trained gardener and freelance landscape architect, founded his own practice in 1970. He defines his method of work in the following way: "My objective is to develop spatial compositions and design qualities which attain a high level of implicitness, which are right for the respective locations, which reach people to satisfy their needs for usage and for experience, create a good mood and also carry a musical component."

above:
New building, villa and sculpture by Bernar Venet
below:
New Heidehof Bosch building
by Professor Kulka

Project Facts
Builder-owner: Robert Bosch GmbH
Building Time: 2002–2004
Size: 24,500 m²

above left:
Aerial photograph showing
overall constellation
above right:
Grove of sycamores with view
of the town and look-out
terrace in the park

below left:
Site plan of park, villa and
new building
below right:
Villa and extended lake

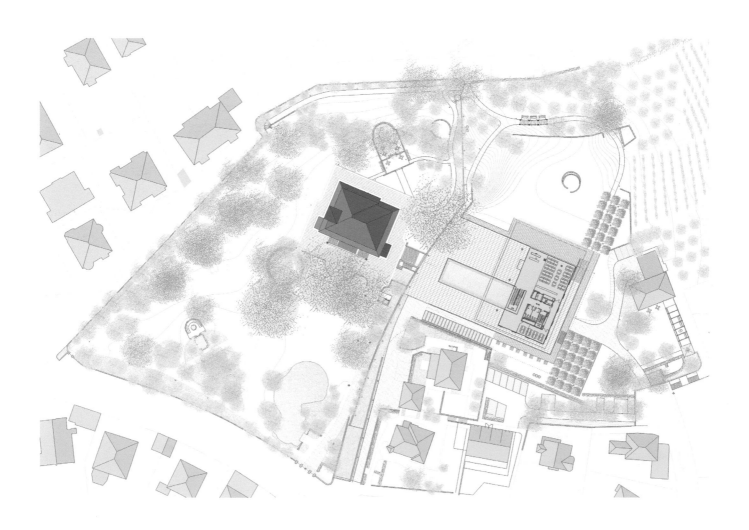

Wartner & Zeitzler

These two graduate landscape architects aim to promote a clear formal language with a high quality of detail. Increasingly their aim is a conservational approach to soil and water. On the occasion they are in close contact with specialists of other disciplines to develop cost-efficient, ecological optimised and social effective solutions.

City-Center Landshut Outdoor Development

Landshut

Because it is heavily built up on all four sides, this site in the heart of Landshut, covering some 10,400 square metres, is surrounded by only a relatively small strip of pavement. Along the eastern and southern facades strips of concrete slabs alternate with strips of small-stone paving. Otherwise the dominant components are quiet surfaces of granite pavement, set in rows and in the Passée style. Along the south side a special granite trim allows public-transport vehicles to drive on the pedestrian paths later. Twenty-two closely planted robinias surround the building complex like a "curtain", creating a peaceful, green framework. ❙ A particular characteristic of this development is the greening and use of roof surfaces. The roof greening, covering some 5,800 square metres – about 55 per cent of the roof surface – was added as a measure for ecological balance, since the entire property had earlier been completely sealed. ❙ The roof terrace, covering around 1,850 square metres on the second floor of the City-Center, is paved with concrete slabs, placed on pallets. Fifteen serviceberries in watered stone tubs, with their splendid blossom in spring and rich colouring in autumn, provide a striking colour-scheme for the whole year. The strict matrix of 8 by 8 metres within which the plant tubs have been set ensures a clear arrangement of space, with a graphic effect. During the summer months the terrace serves as a sheltered beer garden over the roofs of Landshut.

above:
Spacious roof greening and terrace of severe geometric form for catering and recreation (bird's eye view)
below:
A small number of materials provide an exciting contrast

Project Facts
Builder-owner: City-Center Landshut Projektentwicklungsgesellschaft mbH
Building Time: 2002–2003
Size: 10,400 m²
Architects: Otto Steidle + Partner, Architects BDA with
ATP Achhammer – Tritthart & Partner GmbH

above left:
Robinias mark the public
street area
above right:
Flowering serviceberries on
the roof terrace
below:
Detail of trough and detail of
animal market

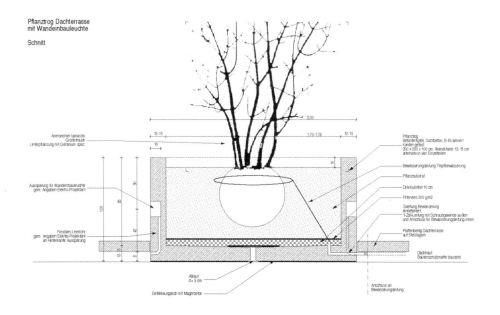

Pflanztrog Dachterrasse
mit Wandeinbauleuchte

Schnitt

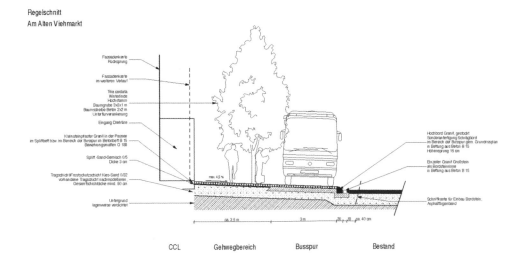

Regelschnitt
Am Alten Viehmarkt

CCL   Gehwegbereich   Busspur   Bestand

above left:
Spectacular autumnal
colouring in the plant tubs
above right:
Pixelled winter view of the
roofscape – tubs and paving
stones in a strict grid
below:
Overview

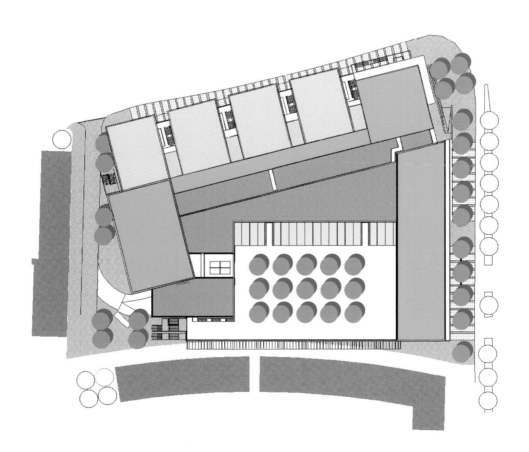

Wolfgang Hermann Niemeyer

Outside Area of the Technical City Hall

Munich

Framed by the clearly structured metal and glass facades of this seven to eight story building (architects: Ganzer & Unterholzner), the character of the grounds of this munipical administration building are governed by the surrounding architecture. The landscape design of the interior courtyard continues the building's message – this open space follows strictly geometric rules and is clearly structured. ❙ More than 80 newly planted trees reflect the axes of the building, thus providing a connection between the interior and the exterior; the glass-roofed entrance hall, extending over eight storeys, is continued in the outside grounds by a roof of plane trees; linear strips of hedge achieve a space-creating effect, defining routes within the closed garden courtyard. The connection with the architecture is made almost palpable through an installation by the New York artist Vito Acconci, entitled "Courtyard in the Wind." ❙ The dominating angle of view in the courtyard, a twenty-story tower marking the north-western corner of the almost rectangular site, is linked with the grounds. The power supplied by a windmill mounted on the tower moves a landscape ring in the inner courtyard, making trees, pavement, benches and lights revolve completely once an hour. The installation is part of the design intention – to make anyone looking out of the numerous office windows perceive the courtyard as a conscious image. To set the exterior space in different levels, all the roofs – some of which can be seen from the upper storeys – have been extensively, some intensively greened.

"Less is more – creative landscape architecture as it relates to architecture" is the guiding concept of this landscapearchitecture practice, founded in 1985. Wolfgang Niemeyer is also engaged in widening the concepts of his discipline: thus language, and particularly music, in the form of sound arrangements and sound installations in open spaces, are becoming a constituent part of landscape architecture.

above:
Landscape in the wind: trees pavement, grass, benches and lamps revolve
below:
Hedges and grass: stillness and movement

Project Facts
Builder-owner: Hannover Leasing (HANKO), Munich
Building Time: 2002–2000
Size: 1.5 ha

above left:
Pillars and trunks – blue and
green roof
above right:
Artistic garden design in the
inner courtyard
below:
Open-space design

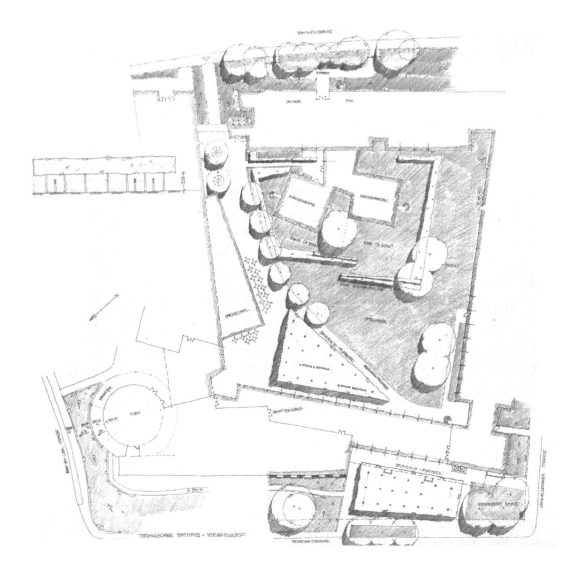

above left:
Roof terrace with Chinese wis-
teria
above right:
Main entrance – roof of
plane trees
below:
Design: roof greening

Martha Schwartz Partners and Peter Kluska

Administration Building Swiss Re

Munich

The open spaces around the Swiss Re office building (architects: Bothe Richter Teherani) is a structural composition which has been fitted into a spatially-articulating architecture. I The central areaway has been made a spatial experience through ponds with four terraces and artificial colour elements. The four quadrants, each of which is designed in one of the primary colours, have been paved with coloured glass mosaic and provided with individual components of an equally colourful kind: yellow natural stones, blue glass cubes and steel boxes filled with green glass shavings. I The gardens, with their strip structure, are also part of the colour design; the bushes, roses, garden and wild shrubs have been selected for the colouration of their flowers, fruits and leaves, so that the primary colours of the individual zones can be recognised at every season. A further feature is provided by light slits into the underground garage in each of the quadrant colours, which at night provide a pattern visible from a distance. I A major architectural feature is the "floating hedge", which forms the main characteristic of the space and includes all parts of the building. A surrounding upright of steel net is covered over all its surface with glycinia and Virginia creeper, creating a characteristic element of design for the building. The overgrowth extends over 4 by 160 metres, with a height of 17 metres. The inner garden area, which has a highly developed design, is surrounded by an outside park. It is formed by groups of trees, which define different areas, and by broad meadows and lawns, which are open to the public.

MSP was formed in 1990. Martha Schwartz is a landscape architect and artist with a major interest in urban projects and the exploration of new design expression in the landscape. Her goal is to find opportunities where landscape design solutions can be raised to a level of fine art. Martha Schwartz is also Visiting Professor of Landscape Architecture at the Harvard University Graduate School of Design.

Peter Kluska, a trained gardener and freelance landscape architect, founded his own practice in 1970. He defines his method of work in the following way: "My objective is to develop spatial compositions and design qualities which attain a high level of implicitness, which are right for the respective locations, which reach people to satisfy their needs for usage and for experience, create a good mood and also carry a musical component."

above:
Floating hedge
below:
Shrub beds in the yellow
square

Project Facts
Builder-owner: Swiss Re Germany AG, Munich
Building Time: 1999–2002
Size: 5.6 ha
39,500 m² (ground greening), 5,700 m² (roof greening)

above left:
Water and coloured art
structures in the inner
courtyard
right:
Colour structures in the
squares

below left:
Site plan with space and
colour structures

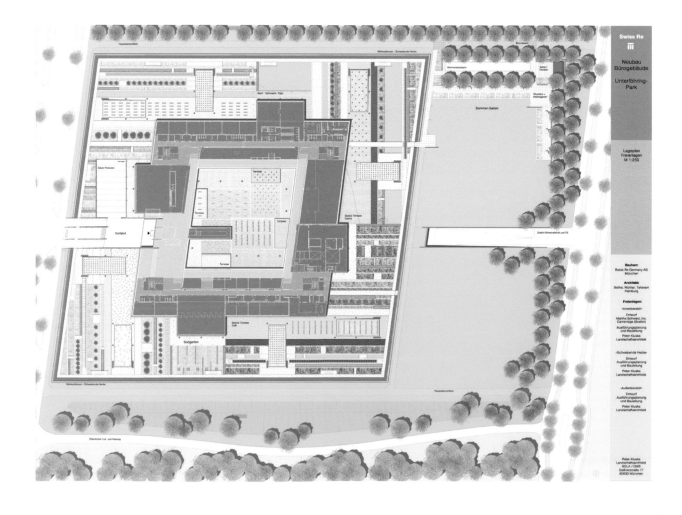

Vogt Landscape Architects

Outside Area of the Allianz Arena

Munich

Mimesis: with the design of the surroundings for the new football stadium (architects Herzog & de Meuron), a new landscape was created in the northern suburbs of Munich. Buildings and landscaping architecture affect each other. The stadium itself will become part of the cityscape and is the fulcrum between nature and art. Together with the topographical portrayal, it reflects the surrounding landscape – the heath Fröttmaninger Heide. For its part, this heath landscape shows the face of a cultural landscape and not a natural landscape. I The central element of the outside area is the 35,000 square metres roof planting on the underground car park which as an esplanade leads the visitors to the stadium. The arched platform is reached from the underground station, the southern coach park and via 6 staircases from the parking floor. It is covered with curved, diagonally crossing paths, the asphalt colour of which matches the plant sub-layer and suggests a uniform covering. I The form and dimensions of the development respect the different use at different times: the stream of spectators to the stadium is considerably staggered during the match by the length and the curved paths. In addition, the esplanade acts as a waiting area in the sense of a public park. The selection of plants takes the surrounding heath landscape as an example, which comprises a mosaic of different vegetation. I The mixture of landscape and park is not only designed as a platform for the new stadium but also as an offensive contribution to the current evaluation of the concept Park.

The Vogt landscape-architecture practice was created in 2000 from Kienast Vogt and Partners. Günther Vogt regards urban nature as the subject and medium of their daily work. They develop programmes and designs from the task in hand and the specific context of a site. Vogt Landscape Architects undertake interdisciplinary dialogue; collaboration with architects, artists and professional planners is regarded as very important.

above:
The Esplanade, in the style of the Fröttmaniger Heide, consists of a mosaic of different types of vegetation
below:
Access point to the football stadium: the roof of the biggest garage-parking facility in Europe, with 11,000 spaces

Project Facts
Builder-owner: Allianz Arena Munich Stadium GmbH
Building Time: 2004–2005
Size: 16 ha

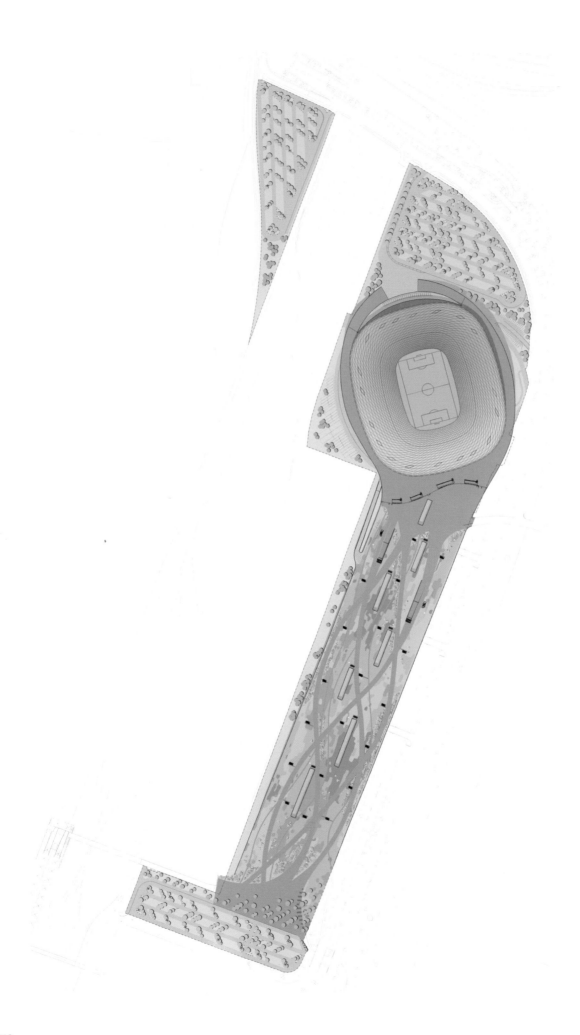

left and right:
The network of curved paths
equalises the stream of spectators as they approach the
Stadium. The ends of the diagonal paths remain hidden
through their interlaced construction

Rainer Schmidt Landscape Architects

Munich Airport, Terminal 2

Munich

Terminal 2 of Munich Airport is situated parallel to Terminal 1 and like its neighbour is of linear design. The Munich Airport Center provides the link between the two. I The design of the grounds around the building required that high tech airport building (K+P Architects and Town Planners) be given its own character, one that exceeded that of a purpose-built, functional building. Departing and arriving passengers were to be provided with a picture of the region, hence the care taken with the stylised depictions of the Bavarian natural and cultural landscape – the Munich gravel plain, the willows in the foothills of the Alps and the outcrops and gravel areas of the Alps themselves. I The result was, among other things, an area of large pebbles adorning the ground outside the central building and reminiscent of the gravel bed of the river Isar. Pines dot the area along with vegetation recalling the growth along the banks of the river that meanders through the Munich gravel plain. The trees are arranged in a more orderly fashion where they line the approach to the hall; the dominating image here is of the architectural equivalent of the tree-lined avenue, a common feature in the grounds of many stately homes of the region. Beneath the bridges rockeries have been created to represent an alpine landscape, a gravel area interspersed with rough boulders. I The roof of the southern underground car park features a special homage to the hilly landscape of the alpine approaches – geometric sections of turf arranged in opposing rows represent the hills, which are decked with rocky outcrops at staggered intervals. In this heavily built-up environment the garden is an inviting place to spend time. Its hills screen people almost perfectly from the cars using the underground garage whilst the drivers descending into the parking facility enjoy a characterful entrance in a setting reminiscent of the grounds of a stately home.

The philosophy of the business, founded in 1991, is to find answers to the problems of our times, aware that the landscape architecture of the twenty-first century should be a realistic reflection of how people come to terms with each other and with nature. Rainer Schmidt attempts to realise these answers in designs, thus finding a balance between design, functions and feelings.

above:
Flowering amelanchier and broad lawns above the garages
below:
Geometrical lawn segments as homage to the hilly countryside of the Alpine foreland

Project Facts
Builder-owner: Munich Airport Baugesellschaft mbH
Building Time: 2000–2003
Size: 12 ha
Architects:
K+P Architects and Town Planners

above left:
Forecourt to Terminal 2 and
Plaza of MAC Munich Airport
Center
below left:
Master plan for Terminal 2
right:
Lawn segments in opposed
rows complete the play with
clear geometrical forms

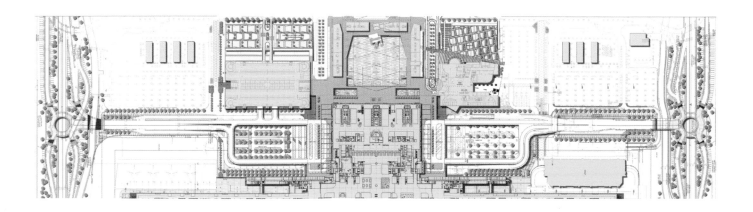

Irene Burkhardt Landscape Architects

Research and Competence Center for Construction Chemicals

Trostberg

The new research center's alignment enters into a direct dialogue with the old town of Trostberg. Located on the verges of the company site, it was possible to retain the existing old director's building and an adjoining park. I The concept design for the open spaces was developed in close cooperation with the architects Raupach & Schurk. Interiors and open spaces are closely intertwined. Plantings, terraces and plazas are aligned in parallel bands both in- and outside the building's glass shell. Temperature and light conditions inside the protective shell were engineered to provide a mediterranean climate, allowing for lush plantings with a wide range of plant species from all over the world. I In reference to the client's role as a global player, one part of the building was designed with Old World, the other with New World species. While the more exposed roofs carry dry tolerant vegetation, the plantings become more luxuriant in the lower floors. The entrance foyer is designed with plants from the warm temperate forests of Eastern Asia. Feature trees are camphor laurel and magnolias. I Temporary open grounds to the back of the building will serve as recreational spaces for employees until further extension of the research center. They are planted with fields of species that provide renewable primary products, such as poplars, willows and reeds. I Mediterranean plants that provide scents, resins, dyes and other resources were also planted, some of them both inside and outside: lavender, roses, woodruff, saffron and madder as well as trees such as pines and liquidambar.

Irene Burkhardt (*1952 worked from 1988 to 1991 in the City of Munich Planning Department, in charge (among other things) of preparing and holding the city-planning and countryside competition for news ideas, entitled "Re-using the Munich-Riem Airport Site." She was engaged as a permanent consultant on ecology for the Riem development scheme as a freelance, followed by founding her own company.

above:
Foyer with plants from Eastern Asia, michelia and campher laurel in the background
below:
View of the glass shell and roof terraces

Project Facts
Builder-owner: degussa construcion chemicals gmbh
Building Time: 2002–2003
Size: 1.5 ha (terrain) + 2,000 m² (interior)
Architects: Raupach and Schurk Architects

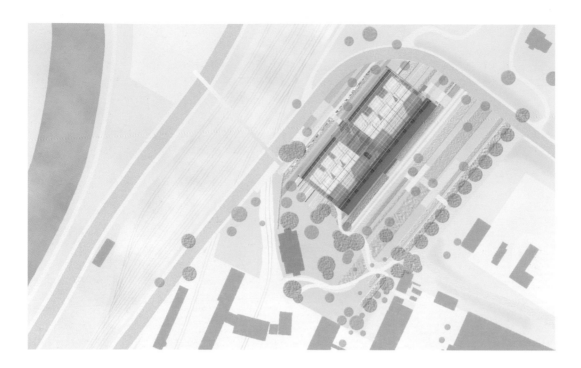

above left:
Competition design showing
the entire site (1999)
above right:
Roofscape showing vegetation
from the New World
below left:
Flowering yucca from the New
World and Mockorange
(Pittosporum) on ground floor
below right:
The drainage area to the front,
designed as a temporary
stream bed as found in the
nearby Alps

Rotzler Krebs Partners

Storage Depot and Park Deck
of Maag-Recycling

Winterthur   The scrap dealer's garden: the big industrial shed lies
between major roads and a canalised river. It is run as
a collection point by a private operator and its function
is to collect, store and treat a wide range of recycling
materials and industrial waste. Its design elements
emphasise the functional character of this industrial
site. The programme is a fusion of the artificially natural and the aesthetic transfiguration of recycling products. I A separate section on the open park deck is used
as a stopping place for staff and passers-by and as a
presentation platform for a wide range of materials.
Seating units, enclosed in wire netting, are filled with
various recycling materials – such as drink cans,
cables, food cans, and plastic; these refer playfully to
the company's business activities. I The bright green
paintwork on the concrete roof serves as waterproof-
ing and represents the "company colour." Ground
lights, traffic markings and signs all suggest runway
lighting at airports. I Magenta-coloured plant tubs of
glass-fibre-strengthened plastic stand as an alienated
industrial product in stark contrast to the bright green
ground colouring. The light, mineral plant substrate
with high water retention is covered with a layer of broken glass. The plants seem to grow directly out of the
recycling material. The tubs are planted with tough,
fast-growing, first-growing shrubs. As the seasons
change, so attention switches to the changing shapes
and colours of the plant species used: the pink blossom of the tamarisk, the violet flowers of the summer
lilac, the "scented cloud" of the smoke tree, the autumnal blood-red of the staghorn.

This planning practice headed by Stefan
Rotzler and Matthias Krebs, has been in
existence since 1990. They work on the
basis of a radical perception of what is
there. They decode situations and problems and develop succinct images from
them, which contain a provocative element through their uncompromising and
unusual combination of things and
themes. This releases energy in in viewers; creates aggression, joy, exitement,
laughter.

above:
Recreation area with plants
below:
Storage depot for
recycling materials

Project Facts
Builder-owner: Max Maag AG
Building Time: 2003–2004
Size: 3,000 m²
Architects: oos ag, Zurich

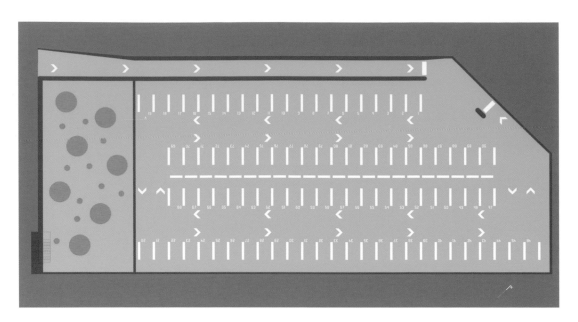

above left:
Ground plan
above right:
Access ramp and parking deck

below left:
Car-park graphics
below right:
Recreation area with seats
made of recycling material

Rotzler Krebs Partners

Zurich-Development-Center

Zurich   The former Bircher-Benner Clinic on the Zurichberg is a place which generates its own atmosphere through the significance of its past history – since it was here over 100 years ago that Dr. Bircher invented the famous "Birchermüesli." Today the whole complex belongs to an international insurance company which has an executive-training center there. The historically important parklands have been restored to reflect legislation on the preservation of heritage gardens and, in collaboration with Henn Architects, adapted to current needs. I Surrounded by trees, the park extends over several steps in the landscape, in levels running parallel to the slope. Each level is marked by a specific type of garden and divided and linked by hedges: seats, promenade walks, wellness-zones, sun-terraces and flower-beds. The lower part of the grounds is designed as an artificial hedge garden: concave and convex hedge walls create a continuous horizon as the terrain falls away and are punctuated by shining windows of colour; coloured embrasures are so arranged as to afford alternate insights and perspectives. This "hedge theatre" invites the visitor to seek forever changing perspectives on his surroundings – or even to become part of the show. I At the park's lowest level a lip-shaped water-basin at the pivotal point of the new structure provides a link between building and park and vitalises the open area of the cafeteria. The idiosyncratic rural architecture of the existing chalets is woven into a scene reminiscent of Alpine foothills, with birch trees planted in clumps. The complement of the forest edge and the incorporation of the rural Wolfbachtobel gives a visual extension to the park. In this once aristocratic garden precise planting ensures that flowers provide accents of colour and bring about a varied and intensive garden experience.

This planning practice headed by Stefan Rotzler and Matthias Krebs, has been in existence since 1990. They work on the basis of a radical perception of what is there. They decode situations and problems and develop succinct images from them, which contain a provocative element through their uncompromising and unusual combination of things and themes. This releases energy in in viewers; creates aggression, joy, exitement, laughter.

above:
Hedge window
below:
Garden to walk in
for managers

Project Facts
Builder-owner: Zurich Financial Services
Building Time: 2000–2001
Size: 11,700 m²
Architects: Aebi + König

above left:
Hedge theatre
above right:
Colourful views
below:
Ground plan

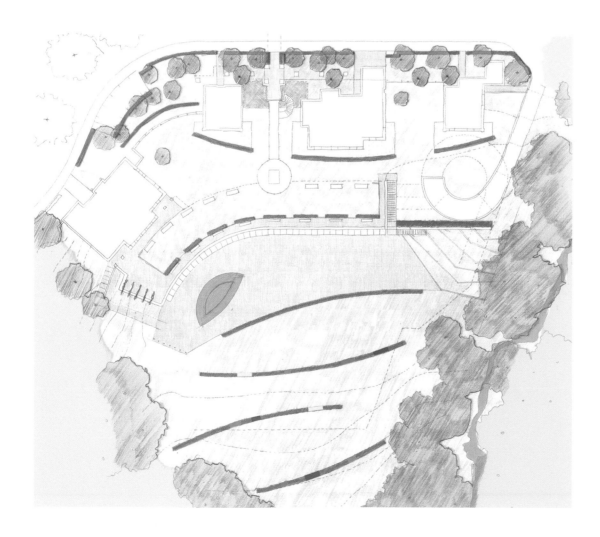

above left:
Water surface
above right:
Hedge window
below:
Axonometrics

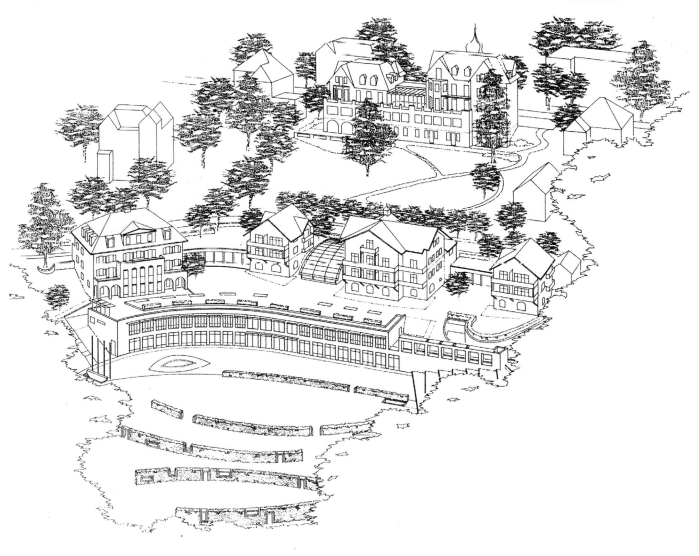

295

rockinger and schneider landscape architecture

Open Spaces of an Apartment Complex, Theresienhöhe South

Munich

The basis of the overall design for the new development in Munich at Theresienhöhe South is the urban development plan, which foresees an open construction with individual point buildings. Despite the open building formation of the four solitary constructions in District WA3, the public and private spaces are clearly differentiated. **I** From the outside, the design of the transitions from the public road spaces to the commonly used courtyard is the defining theme. Pedestal walls up to 60 cm high surround the construction district. Cut privet hedges and small-blossoming trees edge the space without closing it off. As the courtyard is up to one metre above street level, there remains a free view over the surrounding area. **I** The generous courtyard has different accommodation areas. A square, shaded by robinia, defines the center of the courtyard. In the west and east there are smaller squares with play areas as well as seating areas under two pergolas. Caterpillar stairs and access lead from the north and south to the courtyard. They are accompanied by offset plantings from willows and herbaceous shrubs. The plants are space-forming and dividing elements. **I** Concrete, wood and steel are consciously used exclusively. As a result of the reduced number of materials and colours, the overall development can be perceived as a unit – this also includes buildings. The material of the pedestal walls which surround the development is used in the pedestal plates of the buildings. The sand-coloured walls, grit and gravel around the building correspond to the clean facades and contrast the dark-grey concrete layers, steps and walls inside the development.

Both owners founded their practice in 2000 in Munich. In their planning they want to initiate developments surpassing the defined limits of the project. The changing times of day and seasons, the growth of plants and the enabling of social interaction are just a few of the dynamic parameters of the open space. A clear formal language and a solid basic structure are giving the frame for this development of worthwhile open spaces.

above:
Wooden deck on the
sand-play area
mid:
Courtyard center, shaded by
robinias
below:
The residential buildings are
grouped round the communal
courtyard

Project Facts
Builder-owner: Wohnungsgenossenschaft Munich West e.G.
Building Time: 2004
Size: 2,850 m²
Architects: b17 Architects . Kühleis . de la Ossa . Partnership

above:
A place to stop under the
pergola
below left:
Wooden sections divide the
sand-play area
below right:
Walls and corners form a wide
variety of spaces.
right:
View and ground plan

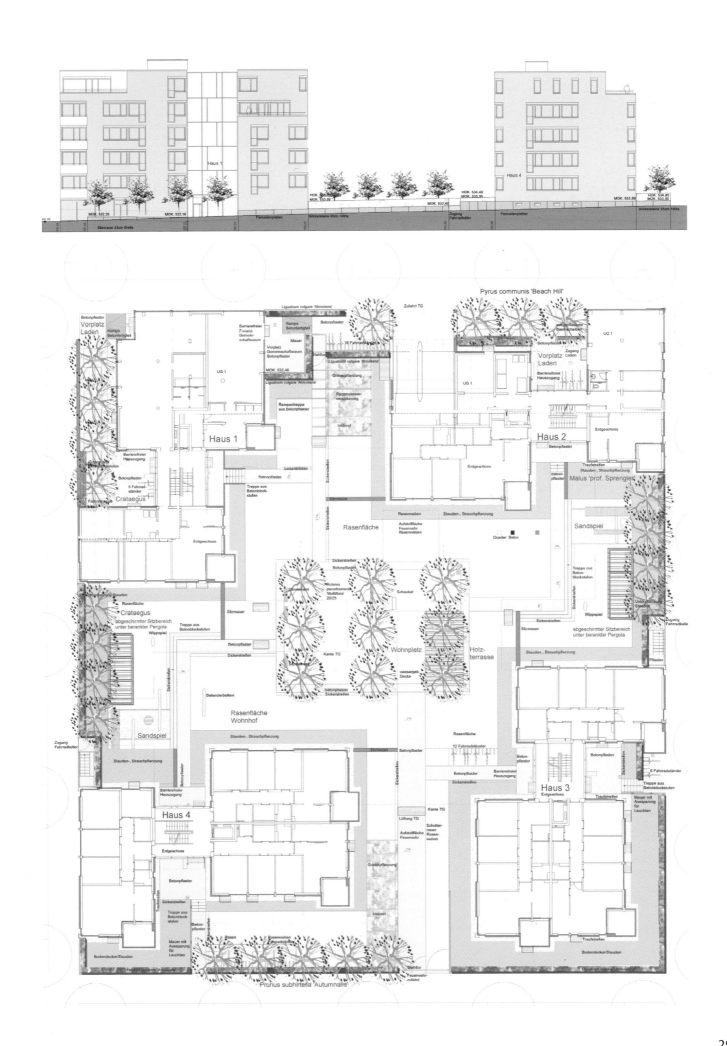

Pyrus communis 'Beach Hill'

Vorplatz
Laden

Ligustrum vulgare 'Atrovirens'

Rampe
Betonfertigtl

Mauer

Barrierefreier
Zugang
Gemein-
schaftsraum

Betonpflaster

Zufahrt TG

Betonpflaster

16 Fahrradständer

Vorplatz
Laden

Zugang
Laden

Vorplatz
Gemeinschaftsraum
Betonpflaster

Stahltor

UG 1

Barrierefreier
Hauszugang

MOK 532,46

Ligustrum vulgare 'Atrovirens'

Gräserpflanzung

Ligustrum vulgare 'Atrovirens'

Rampentreppe
aus Betonpflaster

Regenwasser-
versickerung

Haus 1

Barrierefreier
Hauszugang

Erdgeschoss

Haus 2

Betonpflaster

UG 1

Barrierefreier
Hauszugang

5 Fahrrad-
ständer

Crataegus

Erdgeschoss

Betonpflaster

Sickerstreifen

Trittsteinpflaster

Sickerstreifen

Erdgeschoss

Treppe aus
Betonblock-
stufen

Stauden-, Strauchpflanzung

Malus 'prof. Sprengler'

Rasenfläche

Rasenwaben

Aufstellfläche
Feuerwehr
Rasenwaben

Stauden-, Strauchpflanzung

Sandspiel

Quader Beton

Sitzmauer

Sickerstreifen
Betonpflaster

Treppe mit
Beton-
blockstufen

Robinia
pseudoacacia
'Multiflora'
20/25

Schaukel

Crataegus

Rasenfläche

abgeschirmter Sitzbereich
unter beranktn Pergola

Wippspiel

Treppe aus
Betonblockstufen

Schaukel

Wippspiel

Wohnplatz

Betonpflaster

Kante TG

wassergeb.
Decke

Holz-
terrasse

Sitzmauer

abgeschirmter Sitzbereich
unter beranktn Pergola

Stauden-, Strauchpflanzung

Pflaster

Zugang
Fahrradkeller

Sitzmauer

Betonpflaster
Sickerstreifen

Balancierbalken

Rasenfläche
Wohnhof

Stauden-, Strauchpflanzung

Zugang
Fahrradkeller

Sandspiel

Stauden-, Strauchpflanzung

Betonpflaster

Barrierefreier
Hauszugang

Rasenfläche

12 Fahrradständer

Betonpflaster

Barrierefreier
Hauszugang

Betonpflaster

Betonpflaster

5 Fahrradständer

Sickerstreifen

Sickerstreifen

Haus 3

Erdgeschoss

Traufstreifen

Mauer mit
Aussparung
für
Leuchten

Haus 4

Erdgeschoss

Kante TG

Lüftung TG

Aufstellfläche
Feuerwehr
Rasenwaben

Schotter-
rasen
Rasen-
waben

Betonpflaster

Treppe aus
Betonblock-
stufen

Betonpflaster

Sickerstreifen

Gräserpflanzung

Traufstreifen

Schotter-
rasen

Mauer mit
Aussparung
für
Leuchten

Rasen

Rasenwaben

Bodendecker/Stauden

Stahltor

Feuerwehr-
zufahrt

Bodendecker/Stauden

Prunus subhirtella 'Autumnalis'

Haus 1

Haus 4

MOK. 532,25

MOK. 532,16

Fassadenplatten

Winkelsteine 65cm Höhe

Sitzmauer 33cm Breite

HOK 533,05
MOK. 533,05

Zugang
Fahrradkeller

MOK. 533,40

Fassadenplatten

Haus 4

HOK. 534,40
MOK. 533,95

MOK. 533,95

Winkelsteine 65cm Höhe

HOK. 534,95
MOK. 533,95

hutterreimann + cejka

On a decent basis of experience and pragmatism the practice works unusual, experimental and future orientated. From the concept to the architectual conversion their collaboration with planning partners and clients is based on economy, quality assurance and flexibility. She sees the quintessence of her work in an overlap between the new and the familiar, between reflection and imagistic poetry.

Vienna Woods Islands

Vienna

The open space around the residential development planed by Schindler + Szedenik Architekten in the alley Seitenberggasse in Vienna is shaped by a strictly right-angled system of surfaces: a multifunctional core zone of tartan links the outer and inner spaces with the main residential development. Strips of lawn form a buffer zone towards the private gardens, which are surrounded by hedges. Herbaceous islands, shaped like elliptical hills, featuring flowerbeds, beech groves and pines, form subsections. I These create the characteristic spatial elements of the design and form spatial units, which include such features as playgrounds for small children, leisure facilities, and rest zones for the inhabitants. The colouring is provided by perennial shrubs and colourful spring, summer and autumn flowerbeds which, together with the trees, create an exciting, changing herbaceous aspect in every season. I The building design in the courtyard is determined in its components by the soft materials of the ground and provides an element of control through the strict linearity of the overall surface. The firewalls on the courtyard facades, with their harmonised colouring and the trellises placed in front of them, form vertical spatial sculptures. I In the same way as the courtyard, the private gardens on the third storey are accentuated by herbaceous islands. On the seventh floor a series of private gardens are adjoined by a swimming pool with a sunbathing area and a sauna garden with a wooden deck. Contact with the outside and the nearly Vienna Woods is provided by the panoramic view on the "Barbecue Terrace", which is a meeting place for inhabitants and their guests.

above and mid:
Islands of vegetation
below:
Anemone island

Project Facts
Builder-owner: B.A.I. – Bauträger Austria Immobilien GmbH
Building Time: 2003
Size: 5,800 m²
Architects: s & s architects

above left:
Wooden deck sauna terrace
with grass island
above right:
Pool
below:
Site plan;
Functional space partition;
Emotional counterpoint;
Vienna Woods island

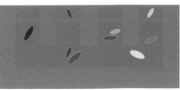

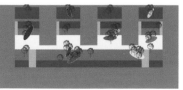

above left:
Pool by night
above right:
Island of grasses by night
below:
Nightscape

Fugmann Janotta – Landscape Architecture and Landscape Development Practice

The Fugmann Janotta practice is engaged in every aspect of open-space and project planning. It focuses on public parks and outside grounds for research institutes and social infrastructure. The collaboration of Harald Fugmann with Martin Janotta in their own practice began in 1986.

New Spa Gardens Bad Saarow

Bad Saarow

After 40 years of shadow existence as a result of the war and the erection of a strictly protected sanatorium for the Soviet army, the new construction of the thermal baths and the restoration of the neighbouring spa gardens will reconnect with the Bad Saarow's golden age in the 1920s and 1930s. I The present design of the open spaces takes up the potential of the site designed in around 1910 by Ludwig Lesser, with its many open spaces and magnificent baths buildings and villas and follows the leitmotif of a representative park characterised by openness, transparency and large-scale. The landscape's qualities, hidden until then – the majestic backdrop of the lake „Scharmützelsee", the gentle topography and the beautiful old trees – are emphasised and the traces clearly left by Ludwig Lesser are taken up. In particular, the contours of the park and the axis are restored through the release of the historic trees. I The sight axes, which reach deep into the site, and the indirect paths in the park or along the bank, make the lake „Scharmützelsee" visible and noticeable. The curved paths in the spa gardens allow the visitor carefully to approach the lake and to see it from different angles. Along the first section of the lake promenade are a pavilion, a lake balcony, spa hall with restaurant terraces and the stairs to the Kurfürstenterrace like a chain of pearls. Alders and willow as well as in part luxuriant reed beds and water plants give this area accents of nature. I For the new design of the open spaces, a timeless and representative design language has been developed with a combination of formal and landscape elements. By contrast, the integrated small buildings such as kiosk, pavilion, pergola and the mobile elements of the park and the materials used are clearly contemporary.

above:
Kurfürstenterraces with footbridge
below:
View over the lake balcony to the Scharmützelsee lake

Project Facts
Builder-owner: Kur- und Fremdenverkehrs-GmbH Bad Saarow
Building Time: 1997–1999
Size: 15 ha

above left:
On the edge of the lake
above right:
Rhododendron grove at the
Moorgraben (moor ditch)

below left:
Location map of the cultivated
areas
below right:
The spa garden is characterised by meadows and an
impressive tree scenery

Freiraumplanung mit System

Gudrun Irrgang and Maik Branzk, both graduates of the TU Dresden, where they also worked as academic assistants, founded the firm in 1993. Their work covers open-space planning (city squares, pedestrian zones, grounds, gardens), landscape planning, maintenance of garden monuments, and regular participation in competitions as well as the work as prize judges.

Johannisbad Spa

Freiberg

As part of Burggraf + Dähne's transformation of the 7,500 square metres former swimming area into a modern bathing facility open all year round the premises have been sub-divided clearly according to function, the sunbathing areas enlarged and the previously separate areas devoted to sports and games have been amalgamated and given a stronger relation to the other parts of the complex. I The character of the bathing facility is designed to reflect the physical link it represents between two neighbouring urban parks: intervening embankments have been levelled out, ramps and plateaux now provide fluid transitions. A stream that had run through a pipe is now an open brook and has become an additional element in the general endeavour to join up the various open-air sections. I The landscape itself has influenced the design of the sports and games areas. A bright blue, undulating surface of smooth, anti-bruise material reflects the surrounding topography, which in turn becomes part of the activities area. Conventional playground features are rejected in favour of a stainless steel hemisphere and an installation composed of four bent stainless steel pipes on a raised sandpit, designed for climbing, sitting and sliding. A climbing wall of white concrete, studded with multicoloured hand and footholds, is apparatus, play-area perimeter, soundproof wall and sculpture in one. I The different sectors are partitioned off from each other by grass borders and white and blue shrubs that form a flowing, wavy pattern on the slopes. This dynamic is continued in elements such as the railings and bike stands and also the benches in the entrance area, designed in the shape of surfboards.

above:
View across the play area to the dome of the swimming pool
below:
View of the bathing pool and the sunbathing area

Project Facts
Builder-owner: Freiberger Bäderbetriebsgesellschaft mbH
Building Time: 2001–2002
Size: 2.5 ha
Architects: Burggraf + Dähne

above left:
Play equipment (detail)
above right:
Forecourt
below:
Plants

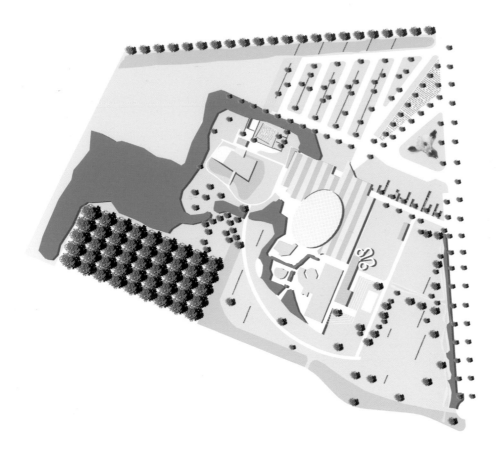

above left:
Site plan
above right:
A re-interpretation of
historical building components as green resting rooms
and ZEN garden

below left:
Sailing into the green sea
below right:
Beach by the sauna pool

Peter Walker and Partners with Rainer Schmidt Landscape Architects

In 1983, Peter Walker founded the firm Peter Walker and Partners Landscape Architecture. Exploring the relationship between art and culture, PWP challenges traditional concepts of design. Their work results from knowledge of history and tradition, sympathy with contemporary needs, understanding of both conceptual and material processes, mastery of construction, and attention to detail.

Kempinski Hotel, Munich Airport

Munich

The Kempinski Hotel of Murphy/Jahn is the first building to be constructed in the section of Munich Airport dubbed the "neutral zone", which forms a counterpoint to the technology-dominated airport area and whose operations revolve firmly around people. I The landscaping concept, underpinning the stylised raised garden, has two patterns set perpendicular to one another in such a way, that their overlap determines the formal, geometric picture of the outside area of the hotel. Since the resulting angles are not a function of the surrounding landscape scale and orientation are conveyed to the observer only by the building's own constructed system. Space is defined by an independent and unified arrangement within which stylistic components of the classical garden and references to the Modern age can relate to each other. I The complex system of lines is traced by low, wide bands of box hedge and cubes of yew. These provide a basic, dominating element that embraces the patches of lawn and reddish brown gravel. Paths of grey stone chippings cross the gardens at regular intervals and tall, slender oak trees, planted in threes, provide a vertical component rising above the geometric pattern on the ground. The complex site can be seen in its entirety from the hotel rooms and offices and from the atrium and hotel terrace too there is a clear view of the linear structures. I Visitors pass through a series of light glass cubes to a hotel entrance flanked by abstract, geometric "trees" forming the curved framework of a wood. Huge glass étagères stand in the hotel entrance and foyer, stacked high with flower pots "planted" with artificial geraniums. A ring of artificial palms by the hotel bar provides a stark contrast to the severe lines of the hotel exterior.

above:
Trimmed hedges flank a covered walkway connecting the hotel with the airport
below:
The paterre garden in front of the hotel

Project Facts
Builder-owner: Munich Airport Baugesellschaft mbH
Building Time: 1997–2000
Size: 1.4 ha

above left:
Paving connects the hotel with
the parterre garden
right:
Palm trees, geranium grids,
and trellis "trees" are among
the primary design elements
below left:
Ligthed paving at the hotel
entrance.

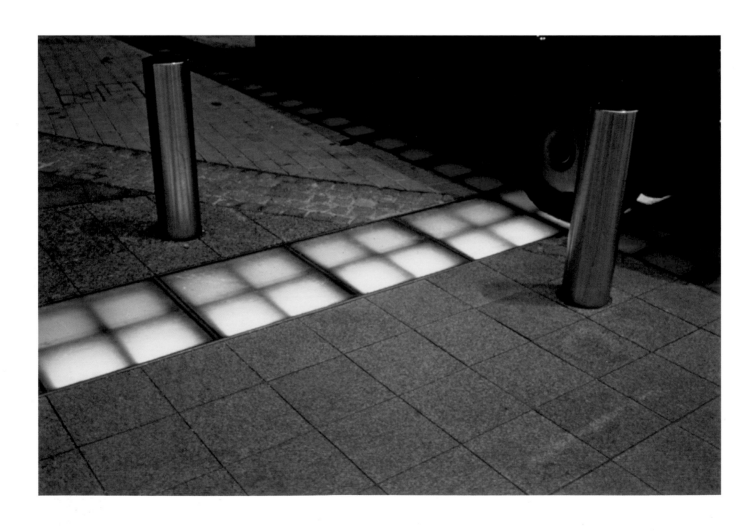

Teutsch Ritz Rebmann Landscape Architects

InterContinental Resort Berchtesgaden

Berchtesgaden

The hotel continues the tradition and culture of tourism at the Obersalzberg from the time before 1933. The aim of the plans was to give the guests at the resort hotel a feeling of the alpine and high-alpine character of the surrounding landscape with its panoramic vistas. In this respect, an important contribution to the design of the open space was the integration of the building and the developments into the landscape. I The external spaces are designed such that the landscape approaches the hotel area. By allowing the high pastures to approach the building, the elevated location is emphasised. The natural stone-covered pedestal storey is carefully integrated into the mountainside with different heights of connection to the land. As a result the hotel does not stand on a separate plateau but instead is inserted into the topography of the mountain according to the slope. I A path around the InterContinental uses the special potential of the location with its rich variety of flora and fauna and makes this an experience on many levels. The existing forest edges are also planted with local bushes and shrubs. Individual groups of trees divide the mountain and integrate the building into the landscape. The path lighting is ground height. This allows the visitor to enjoy the surrounding nature and landscape, even at night. I The roof planting artificially plays with the mountain theme of the high alps through the use of boulders, gravel areas, alpine roses, mountain pines, mountain pasture with typical herbs from the surroundings. The roof terrace of several suites is embedded in this, along with decks which can be used by the hotel guests as viewing platforms or for sunbathing.

This practice, founded in 1961, works in all fields of open-space planning. The range of completed projects runs from outside grounds for administration, hotels and conference buildings, domestic buildings, banks, educational institutions, spa facilities, hospitals, churches and cemeteries, redevelopment of outside facilities, objects of listed garden monuments, to the design of garden shows and sports facilities.

above:
Spa area: terraced lawns with roof terrace
below:
Humid biotope: linear paths and a circular path open up the natural environment and invite the visitor to stay

Project Facts
Builder-owner: Gewerbegrund Obersalzberg GmbH & Co.,
Grundbesitzgesellschaft KG
Building Time: 2004–2005
Size: 5.8 ha
Architect: Kochta Architects, Munich

above left:
Hotel drive, separated trans-
parently from the look-out terraces by tall hornbeams
above right:
View southwards, hotel drive,
Kehlstein and Hoher Göll in the
background

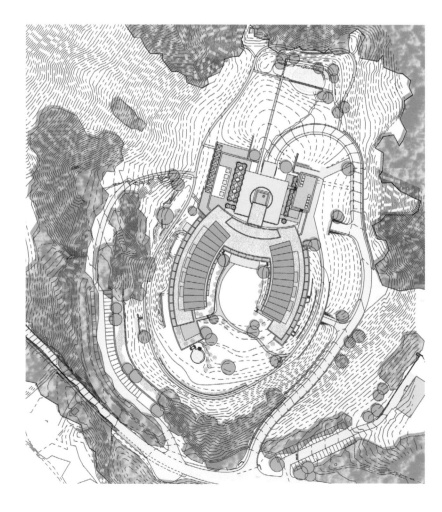

below left:
Site plan
below right:
Circular path and scenic path
on the northern edge of the
forest; mountain meadow with
hill fortification

Vogt Landscape Architects

Masoala Rain Forest Hall, Zoo Zurich

Zurich   Constructed Nature: the giant dimensions (120 metres long, 90 metres wide, up to 30 metres high) of the Masoala Rain Forest Hall in the zoo in Zurich offer possibilities for the original forestation of the low-lying rain forest in Masoala with its unique, characteristic vegetation to be copied. The architectonic constructive shell hides behind the exhibit – behind nature. The visitor does not sense the strongly moved topography of the hall until he walks the entire length of the Rain Forest Hall. ▌ Small paths lead from the main path into the forest-like vegetation. Familiar plants, such as gum trees or dragon trees, have been planted in unusual densities and dimensions. Birds, reptiles and lemurs live here without the otherwise typical frames or cages. The looking-glass principle, often used in zoos or botanical gardens, is removed by direct participation of the visitors as actors. The visitors gain insight into the typical low-laying rain forest. Stalking and climbing paths lead deep into the forest and invite to investigate individual living spaces more closely. ▌ The process of change is part of the design. Lava rocks instead of earth are the basis for the development of the vegetation, over time leaves and branches will form the rain forest flooring. The various stages of development make it possible to participate in a natural process which only develops over several visits. There are no descriptions or name signs, either about the plants or the animals. The basic principle of the jungle of a multi-layered, luxuriant and unclear collection of plants is intensified by the topography, the waterways and paths. Constantly changing mildew and bloom scents confuse the senses, as does the variety of noises.

The Vogt landscape-architecture practice was created in 2000 from Kienast Vogt and Partners. Günther Vogt regards urban nature as the subject and medium of their daily work. They develop programmes and designs from the task in hand and the specific context of a site. Vogt Landscape Architects undertake interdisciplinary dialogue; collaboration with architects, artists and professional planners is regarded as very important.

above:
The constantly changing scents of mould and flowers confuse the senses
below:
Heat, high humidity and a large amount of rain create a damp cosmos

Project Facts
Builder-owner: Zoo Zurich AG
Building Time: 2001–2003
Size: 1 ha
Further Participants: Gantschi Storrer, Zurich

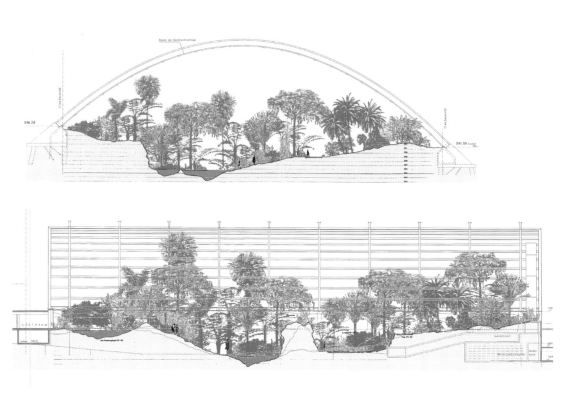

above:
Cross and longitudinal
sections
below and right:
The peep-show principle from
the zoo is replaced by direct
participation in the visits of
the protagonists

Bendfeldt · Schröder · Franke Landscape Architects

Open Spaces of the Domicil Senior Citizens Residence

Through a collaboration between two generations of planners, this practice offers wide experience and innovative ideas for every aspect of open-space and landscape planning. Jens Bendfeldt (*1963) and Uli Franke (*1966) are graduate landscape architects and have been practice partners since 1995. Klaus Schröder (*1946) – working in the practice since 1973 and a partner since 1979 – is also landscape architect.

Kiel   The task for this construction was to create open spaces for senior citizens who want to make use of the benefits of a modern and comfortable apartment in the city. In a protected, almost intimate courtyard not far from the center of Kiel, a small garden oasis has been created as an addition to modern and comfortable old-peoples' apartments. I A concept was developed that allows the garden to have many uses, notably for the residents who can only walk a limited distance. For example, the open space has as few contours as possible in order to be usable for disabled residents. I The courtyard's particular attraction lies mainly the large differences in height, within the small plot. The site's jumps allow it to develop different, fascinating garden areas, even for residents who can only walk a limited distance. I Apart from a small, step-free circular path, a generously proportioned main terrace and other seating in the sun and the shade, there is a steel watercourse as a special element. The water runs from a source pond over a waterfall to the watercourse through the garden and provides a gentle audio backdrop. An aromatic and herb garden with benches, a barbecue and a flower table with wheelchair access in a small area complete the garden for the residents.

above:
Herb and fragrance garden
below:
Large sunny garden terrace

Project Facts
Builder-owner: HBB Hanseatische Bau GmbH, Gesellschaft für Seniorenheime & Co. KG, Lübeck
Building Time: 2003
Size: 460 m²

above left:
Drainpipes with drainage tank
above right:
Large garden terrace with
circular path
below:
Site plan

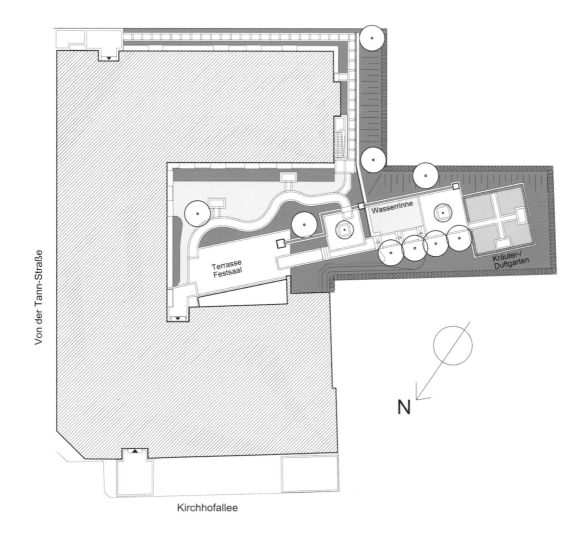

above left:
Small garden terrace
above right:
Splashing waters

below left:
Functional diagram of the
watercourse
below right:
Back view into the courtyard

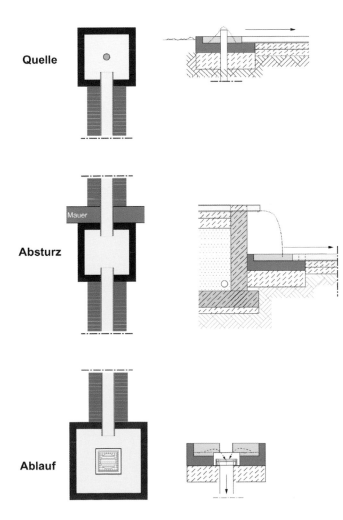

Quelle

Absturz

Mauer

Ablauf

Knippschild & Simons

Landscape architects Elmar Knippschild (*1948) and Paul Simons (*1964) founded their planning practice for garden architecture and construction management in 1997. Its work focuses on planning, project coordination and construction management for open spaces, squares, parks and gardens in city and country.

Center for Dementia Patients – Schönholzer Heide Foundation

Berlin   The Center for Dementia Patients is part of a residential development for senior citizens, designed by Nixdorf Consult. Its grounds are marked by their existing stock of trees, closely incorporated into the structure of restored utilitarian housing from the first part of the twentieth century in a strictly linear way. The grounds open via a central axis, whose end points are marked by two squares. I After the buildings had been restored, the grounds were remodelled, in which process planning the garden posed a particular challenge. The free space must encourage its users – the patients – to find peace, yet it should provide stimulation. To facilitate the need for movement which this illness creates, a circular path was laid out, formed of uniform materials, to avoid causing any confusion through interruptions. I Because dementia patients have a disturbed capacity for orientation, it was necessary to enclose the entire site. To avoid creating a feeling of imprisonment, the enclosures are as unobtrusive and uniform as possible, consisting of a two-row, winter-green privet hedge. The hedge divides up the individual garden areas and organises the sequence of "green rooms" – a sort of extension to the living rooms. Each of these garden rooms is designed on one theme and can be perceived by various senses – the flower and fragrance rooms provide olfactory stimulus through strongly flowering plants, while in another area there are pines and forest grasses, combined with touch stones and a bird bath. I Colour highlights in the area come from so-called "petals", small gardens in the form of roses and hortensias, which also serve as an aid to orientation in the grounds. These beds are planted in collaboration with the people living in the buildings, thus enabling them to take an active part in designing their environment.

above:
Kitchen herbs and soup-making vegetables grow on the plant tables
mid:
The tank of Corten steel fits in naturally with the space
below:
Rhododendrons frame the fountain

Project Facts
Builder-owner: Schönholzer Heide Foundation
Building Time: 2001–2002
Size: 2,300 m²

above left:
The terrace by the tank is the
most popular meeting place in
the garden
above right:
Falling leaves stand out
against the Corten steel
below:
Bird's-eye views

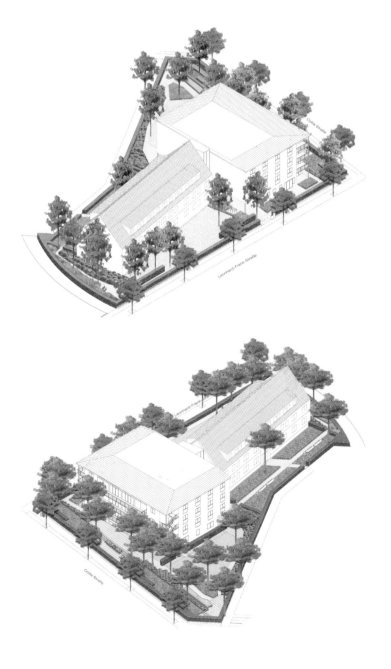

above left:
The various garden spaces
open via a water-bounded
path
above right:
Reflections in a water basin
below:
Site plan

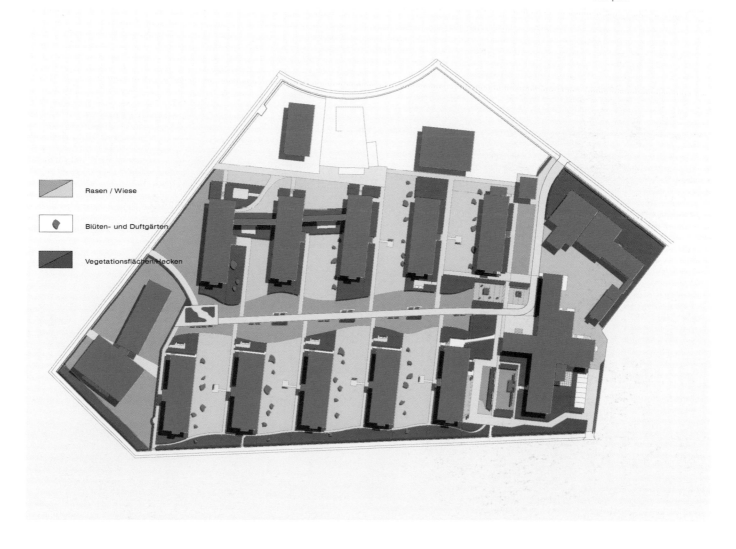

Rasen / Wiese

Blüten- und Duftgärten

Vegetationsflächen/Hecken

Wolfgang Färber Freiraumplanung

Wolfgang Färber studied graphic design and landscape architecture and founded his own practice in 1982. The aim of his planning is to give some quality of life to people in the most varied aspects of life. A major aspect of this is a dialogue with the four elements – earth, water, air + light – producing the familiar, the surprising, the exciting, the relaxing, and sometimes even something totally new.

Hospital of the Brothers of Charity

Munich

The Hospital of the Brothers of Charity, directly adjacent to the Nymphenburg Castle rondelle, has undergone a general restoration since 1989, carried out in a number of stages. In designing the clinic's outside grounds – a green belt adjoining the rondelle – the overriding aim was to preserve the existing trees, whose layout and maintenance are subject to statutory protection. The green belt was therefore carefully converted into park-like areas of patients' gardens, and the guiding principle of the building – "quality of life in illness" – put into expression in its grounds. I A spacious patients' garden provides recreational qualities with a high experiential and recovery value: in the shadow of the huge trees, on carefully designed seats, with water features and a flower bed with segmented shrubs, the patients find peace in harmony with nature. In the two interior courtyards a terrace and a balcony provide an opportunity to sit in the open air. In the area of the hospice ward, too, there are open-air seats and garden areas, designed like winter gardens, in front of the patients' rooms. A pergola, based on the idea of a surrounding cloister, makes it possible to sit out in the open even when it is raining. I In 2003 an extension building was constructed in the clinic's grounds, to plans by architects Kochta, Schimer, Schrader. Its 12 by 11 metres interior light well features a countryside motif across five storeys, in the shape of a grass sculpture. An aquarium with artificial ornamental fish in front of a Plexiglas wall completes the installation, providing a soundscape and a pleasant microclimate with a bright, friendly atmosphere. I The 1,400 square metres roof garden features a steel foliage-covered pergola and a shady roof of snowy-mespilus leaves. Colour highlights come here from the extensive roof lawn, designed as a flower meadow, and from troughs of scented herbs.

above:
Sculpture of grasses,
upper floor
mid:
Light shaft construction
stage 3
below:
Entrance drive to the hospice

Project Facts
Builder-owner:
Hospital of the Brothers of Charity
Building Time: 2002–2003
Size: 8,500 m²
Architects: Kochta, Schirmer, Schrader

above left:
Flowering roof garden in June
above right:
Roof garden construction
stage 3
below:
Site plan of roof garden with
seats and mobility-
rehabilitation center, plus
inner courtyard

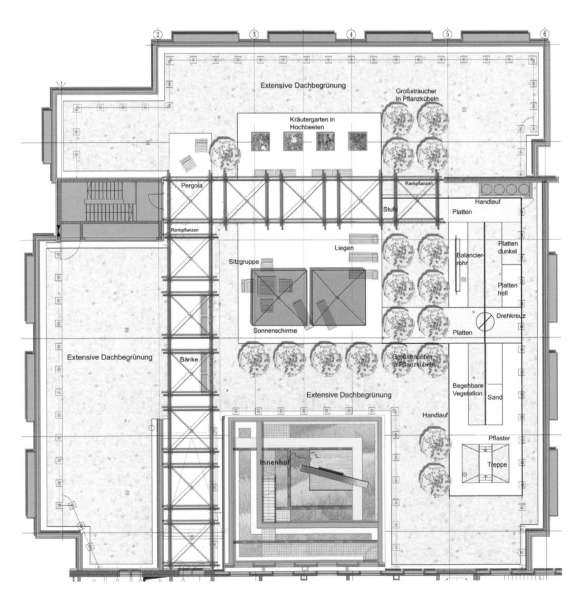

338

above left:
Flowering plants on the
greened roof in July
above right:
Detail of mobility-
rehabilitation center

below:
Seating area in the roof
garden; roof garden at the
height of the trees in the
surrounding park

freiraumarchitektur

Christoph Wey and Markus Bieri studied landscape architecture at Rapperswil. The freiraumarchitektur practice has been engaged since 1994 in open-space planning, garden design and landscape aesthetics. They intend their work to maintain the beauty of the environment and to counteract the monotonisation of the variety of experience. Their work covers project planning, landscape design and landscape aesthetics.

Kneippism Facility Schwandalpweiher

Flühli-Sörenberg

The countryside of Flühli-Sörenberg, being the central zone of the Entlebuch UNESCO Biosphere Reservation, has achieved international status as a model nature protection area. The local tourist authority of Flühli-Sörenberg regards this designation as a challenge to develop strategies, not only for telling tourists about the beauty of the countryside, but to ensure that the region is protected and maintained. It was against this background that the project "Flühli-Water" was created, the aim of which is to promote sustainable development of the culture and countryside of this region in everything connected with water. I Construction of the Schwandalpweiher Kneipp water center in summer 2003 – UNO declared this year "the year of water" – created a foundation for developing the Flühli-Sörenberg countryside water parks. The plan here is to offer new facilities for health and recreation, featuring the therapeutic power of water. I The entrance to the Kneipp water center in a dell above the village of Flühli features a striking stone wall. Once inside the Kneipp landscape, which through its selection of materials – local natural stone and white deal – fits well into the picture of its surroundings, the visitor climbs a stone staircase and reaches an initial platform. At this point the change in the floor covering from stone to wood marks the transition to the center's barefoot area. Wooden stairs lead to platforms devoted to the various different applications of Kneipp health and fitness teachings. Different installations, such as a whirlpool and a water prism, demonstrate the physical phenomena of water.

above:
Carefully fitting the development into the mature landscape – one of the main objectives in the design
mid:
View over the pond to the wading pool
below:
Only natural materials from the immediate vicinity were used to build the complex

Project Facts
Builder-owner: Cooperative Flühli-Wasser
Building Time: 2003
Size: 4,500 m²

above:
The wading platform stretches
into the middle of the pond
mid:
Montage of the idea behind
the Kneipp project
below:
Rest platform over the brook
which feeds the pond

above left:
The dialogue between architecture and the open country
– a recurring theme
above right:
Stairways of wood link the
individual platforms
below:
General view of the complex

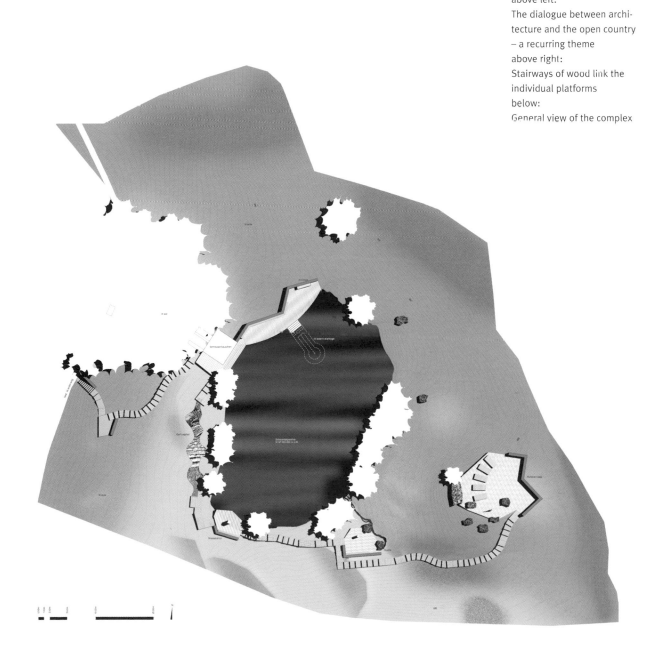

Architects Index

archiscape
Architects and Landscape Architects

→ 170

Wallstrasse 37
D-10179 Berlin
T +49.30.53216350
F +49.30.53216351
welcome@archiscape.de
www.archiscape.de

Auböck + Kárász
Landscape Architects and Architects
Maria Auböck · János Kárász

→ 190

Bernardgasse 21
A-1070 Vienna
T +43.1.5237220
F +43.1.52379676
office@auboeck-karasz.at
www.auboeck-karasz.at

B. A. E. R.
Architects Landscape Architects Engineers

→ 236

Spitzenstrasse 2
D-60437 Frankfurt am Main
T +49.6101.403760
F +49.6101.403762
mail@b-a-e-r.com
www.b-a-e-r.com

bauchplan).(
baldauf . otto . okresek
landscape architecture

→ 24

Kirchstetterngasse 60
A-1160 Vienna
T +43.1.9291333
F +43.1.9291760
buero@bauchplan.de
www.bauchplan.net

Becker Giseke Mohren Richard
Landscape Architects
bgmr Landscape Architects

→ 170

Prager Platz 6
D-10779 Berlin
T +49.30.2145959-0
F +49.30.2145959-59
berlin@bgmr.de
www.bgmr.de

BIERBAUM.AICHELE.landscape architects
Klaus Bierbaum · Klaus-Dieter Aichele

→ 52, 96

Untere Zahlbacher Strasse 21
D-55131 Mainz
T +49.6131.66925-0
F +49.6131.66925-29
info@bierbaumaichele.de
www.bierbaumaichele.de

Landscape Architecture and Urban Development
Bode ▪ Williams + Partners

→ 28

Meraner Strasse 42
D-10825 Berlin
T +49.30.4439290
F +49.30.4439292
bwp@snafu.de
www.bwp-landscapearchitects.com

Bendfeldt · Schröder · Franke
Landscape Architects

→ 36, 328

Jungfernstieg 44
D-24116 Kiel
T +49.431.99796-0
F +49.431.99796-99
bendfeldt@bsf-ki.de
www.bsf-ki.de

Burger Landscape Architects
Susanne Burger

→ 64, 124

Rosenheimer Strasse 139
D-81671 Munich
T +49.89.49000925
F +49.89.49000926
buero@burgerlandschaftsarchitekten.de
www.burgerlandschaftsarchitekten.de

Irene Burkhardt Landscape Architects

→ 284

Fritz-Reuter-Strasse 1
D-81245 Munich
T +49.89.82085540
F +49.89.82085549
info@irene-burkhardt.de
www.irene-burkhardt.de

Därr Landscape Architects
Matthias Därr · Sigrun Därr

→ 88

Ernst-Grube-Strasse 1
D-06120 Halle / Saale
T +49.345.55581-0
F +49.345.55581-30
freiraum@la-daerr.de
www.la-daerr.de

DIPOL Landscape Architects
Andy Schönholzer · Massimo Fontana
Christopher T. Hunziker

→ 140

Strassburgerallee 90
CH-4055 Basel
T +41.61.3879059
F +41.61.3879055
mail@dipol.ch
www.dipol.ch

Planning Office Drecker
Landscape Architects + Engineers

→ 158

Bottroper Strasse 6
D-46244 Bottrop-Kirchhellen
T + 49.2045.9561-0
F +49.2045.9561-24
bottrop@drecker.de
www.drecker.de

DS landscape architects
Maike van Stiphout

→ 76

Overtoom 197
NL-1954 HT Amsterdam
T +31.20.5301252
F +31.20.4230627
info@ds.landschapsarchitecten.nl
www.ds.landschapsarchitecten.nl

fagus Fachgesellschaft für Umwelt- und
Stadtplanung with Dirk Seelemann
Landscape-Architecture Practice
→ 206

Hauptstrasse 9
D-04416 Markkleeberg
T +49.341.356790
T +49.341.3567933
info@fagus-leipzig.de · info@lab-seelemann.de
www.fagus-leipzig.de

Wolfgang Färber Freiraumplanung
Landscape Architect

→ 222, 336

Krautgärten 30
D-82057 Icking
T +49.8178.9601-0
F +49.8178.9601-90
mail@la-faerber.de
www.la-faerber.de

freiraumarchitektur
Markus Bieri · Christoph Wey

→ 340

Neustadtstrasse 7
CH-6003 Lucerne
T +41.41.2200616
F +41.41.2200617
info@freiraumarchitektur.ch
www.freiraumarchitektur.ch

Freiraumplanung mit System
Landscape Architects

→ 308

Chemnitzer Strasse 96
D-01187 Dresden
T +49.351.4724064
F +49.351.4724059
FMS.LA@t-online.de
www.fms-la.de

Fugmann Janotta – Landscape Architecture
and Landscape Development Practice BDLA

→ 304

Belziger Strasse 25
D-10823 Berlin
T + 49.30.7001196-0
F + 49.30.7001196-22
buero@fugmannjanotta.de
www.fugmannjanotta.de

GHP Landscape Architects
Gurr · Herbst · Partners

→ 228

Flachsland 27
D-22083 Hamburg
T +49.40.413607-0
F +49.40.413607-11
mail@ghp-landschaftsarchitekten.de
www.ghp-landschaftsarchitekten.de

Atelier Girot
Christophe Girot

→ 72

Postfach 189
CH-8093 Zurich
T +41.43.5404291
F +41.43.2338325
info@girot.ch
www.girot.ch

Gruppe F Landschaftsarchitektur Freiräume
Tho-Mi Bauermeister · Nikolai Köhler ·
Gabriele Pütz
→ 84

Cuvrystrasse 1
D-10997 Berlin
T +49.30.6112334
F +49.30.6112434
info@gruppef.de
www.gruppef.de

GTL Gnüchtel Triebswetter
Landscape Architects
Markus Gnüchtel · Michael Triebswetter
→ 178

Grüner Weg 21
D-34117 Kassel
T +49.561.78946-0
F +49.561.78946-11
kontakt.gtl-kassel.de
www.gtl-kassel.de

Häfner / Jiménez
Landscape Architecture Practice
Winfried Häfner · Thomas Jarosch · Jens Betcke
→ 92

Schwedter Strasse 263
D-10119 Berlin
T +49.30.28391303
F +49.30.28391312
info@haefner-jimenez.de

Architects Index

Hager Landscape Architecture
Guido Hager

→ 136

Bergstrasse 85
CH-8032 Zurich
T +41.1.2549920
F +41.1.2549922
info@hager-ag.ch
www.hager-ag.ch

Hanke + Partners Landscape Architects
Reinhard Hanke · Barbara Hanke ·
Holger Plaasche
→ 80

Fraenkelufer 30
D-10999 Berlin
T +49.30.6146086
F +49.30.6157051
landschaftsarchitekten@hanke-partner.de
www.hanke-partner.de

hutterreimann + cejka Landscape Architecture
Barbara Hutter · Stefan Reimann
Andrea Cejka
→ 202, 300

Möckernstrasse 68
D-10965 Berlin

Albertgasse 13–17
A-1080 Vienna
www.hr-c.net

Jühling and Bertram Landscape Architects
Stefanie Jühling · Otto A. Bertram

→ 112

Bauerstrasse 19
D-80796 Munich
T +49.89.277789-0
F +49.89.277789-99
jue@st-juehling.de · bertram@oabertram.de
www.st-juehling.de · www.oabertram.de

keller landscape architects
Regine Keller · Franz Damm

→ 12

Dachauer Strasse 17
D-80335 Munich
T +49.89.442317-0
F +49.89.442317-13
buero@keller-landschaftsarchitekten.de
www.keller-landschaftsarchitekten.de

BÜRO KIEFER landscape architecture berlin
Gabriele G. Kiefer

→ 198

Mariannenplatz 23
D-10997 Berlin
T +49.30.61709870
F +49.30.61709805
info@buero-kiefer.de
www.buero-kiefer.de

Peter Kluska
Landscape Architect

→ 60, 260, 272

Gassnerstrasse 17
D-80639 Munich
T +49.89.176008
F +49.89.173204
kluska.landschaftsarchitekt@t-online.de

Knippschild & Simons
Landscape Gardening & Site Management

→ 332

Derfflinger Strasse 6
D-10785 Berlin
T +49.30.230995-0
F +49.30.230995-55
office@knippschild-simons.com

Krafft Wehberg Landscape Architects
Henrike Wehberg-Krafft · Hans-Hermann Krafft
→ 232

Üderseestrasse 27
D-10318 Berlin
T +49.30.6141303
F +49.30.618953
kwberlin@t-online.de

Landscape Architecture and Ecology
Angela Bezzenberger

→ 56

An der Eschollmühle 30
D-64297 Darmstadt
F +49.6151.9464-0
F +49.6151.9464-19
info@loek.de
www.loek.de

Latitude Nord Paysagistes
Gilles Vexlard · Laurence Vacherot

→ 182

233-235 avenue du Général Leclerc
F-94700 Maison Alfort
T +33.1.43536470
F +33.1.43536471
latitude.nord@wanadoo.fr

Latz + Partners
Landscape Architects Planners

→ 166

Ampertshausen 6
D-85402 Kranzberg
T +49.8166.6785-0
F +49.8166.6785-33
post@latzundpartner.de
www.latzundpartner.de

Levin Monsigny
Landscape Architects

→ 104

Schönhauser Allee 182
D-10119 Berlin
T +49.30.44053184
F +49.30.44053651
mail@levin-monsigny.com
www.levin-monsigny.com

lohrer.hochrein landscape architects
Axel Lohrer · Ursula Hochrein

→ 120, 132

Bauerstrasse 8
D-80796 Munich
T +49.89.287791-0
F +49.89.287791-29
loho@lohrer-hochrein.de
www.lohrer-hochrein.de

Atelier LOIDL
Gesellschaft von Landschaftsarchitekten und
Ingenieuren
→ 186

Am Tempelhofer Berg 6
D-10965 Berlin
T +49.30.6914785
F +49.30.6919730
office@atelier-loidl.de
www.atelier-loidl.de

atelier loidl–reisch
Cordula Loidl-Reisch

→ 20

Lindengasse 5/7
A–1070 Vienna
T +43.1.5231037
F +43.1.5249089
atelier@loidl-reisch.at
www.loidl-reisch.at

Martha Schwartz Partners
MSP

→ 272

147 Shermann Street, Suite 200
USA–Cambridge, MA 02140
T +1.617.6618141
F +1.617.6618707
msi@marthaschwartz.com
www.marthaschwartz.com

Wolfgang Hermann Niemeyer
Landscape Architect

→ 268

Agnes-Bernauer-Platz 8
D-80687 Munich
T +49.89.587989
F +49.89.587448
WolfgangNiemeyer@t-online.de

Pfrommer + Roeder
Free Landscape Architects
Dieter Pfrommer · Ulf Roeder
→ 256

Humboldtstrasse 6
D-70178 Stuttgart
T +49.711.96003-0
F +49.711.96003-33
kontakt@pfrommer-roeder.de
www.pfrommer-roeder.de

realgrün Landscape Architects
Klaus D. Neumann · Wolf D. Auch

→ 108

Mariahilfstrasse 6
D-81541 Munich
T +49.89.6146580
F +49.89.669513
realgruen.la@t-online.de
www.realgruenlandschaftsarchitekten.de

Rehwaldt Landscape Architects
Till Rehwaldt

→ 174

Bautzner Strasse 133
D-01099 Dresden
T +49.351.8119690
F +49.351.8119699
mail@rehwaldt.de
www.rehwaldt.de

relais Landscape Architects
Gero Heck · Marianne Mommsen

→ 218

Rosenheimer Strasse 7
D-10781 Berlin
T +49.30.23629721
F +49.30.23629722
buero@relaisLA.de
www.relaisLA.de

RMP Landscape Architects
Raderschall · Möhrer · Peters · Lenzen

→ 214

Klosterbergstrasse 109
D-53177 Bonn
T +49.228.952570
F +49.228.321083
info@rmp-landschaftsarchitekten.de
www.rmp-landschaftsarchitekten.de

rockinger und schneider
landscape architecture
Andreas Rockinger · Martina Schneider
→ 296

Wörthstrasse 18a
D-81667 Munich
T +49.89.44489334
F +49.89.44489335
mail@rockingerundschneider.de
www.rockingerundschneider.de

Architects Index

Rotzler Krebs Partners
Landscape Architects BSLA

→ 144, 288, 292

Lagerplatz 21
CH-8400 Winterthur
T +41.52.2690860
F +41.52.2690861
info@rkp.ch
www.rkp.ch

Rainer Schmidt
Landscape Architects

→ 68, 252, 280, 316

Klenzestrasse 57c
D-80469 Munich
T +49.89.202535-0
F +49.89.202535-30
mail@schmidt-landschaftsarchitekten.de
www.schmidt-landschaftsarchitekten.de

Adelheid Schönborn
Landscape Gardener

→ 128

Elisabethstrasse 13
D-80796 Munich
T +49.89.273717-3
F +49.89.273717-47
muenchen@ags-garten.de
www.ags-garten.de

Schupp + Thiel Landscape Architecture
Reiner Thiel

→ 210

Bahnhofstrasse 1-5
D-48143 Münster
T +49.251.662666
F +49.251.662668
info@schupp-und-thiel.de
www.schupp-und-thiel.de

Schweingruber Zulauf
Landscape Architects

→ 154

Vulkanstrasse 120
CH-8048 Zurich
T +41.43.3366070
F +41.43 3366080
info@schweingruberzulauf.ch
www.schweingruberzulauf.ch

Karin Standler
Technical Office for
Landscape Architecture and Horticulture
→ 148

Seidengasse 13/3
A-1070 Vienna
T +43.1.5954549
F +43.1.5954549
standler@chello.at
www.standler.at

stock + partners · Free Landscape Architects
Wolfram Stock · Tim Hofmann

→ 248

Geschwister-Scholl-Strasse 2
D-07749 Jena
T +49.3641.445215
F +49.3641.449361
buero@stock-partner-jena.de
www.stock-partner-jena.de

Stötzer · Neher
Landscape Architects Urban Planners
Engineers
→ 244

Talstrasse 51
D-71069 Sindelfingen
T +49.7031.73251-0
F +49.7031.73251-99
www.stoetzer-neher.de
sindelfingen@stoetzer-neher.de

Teutsch Ritz Rebmann
Landscape Architects

→ 320

Kirchenstrasse 91
D-81675 Munich
T +49.89.41 41 95-0
F +49.89.41 41 95-19
office@la-teutsch.de
www.la-teutsch.de

Thomanek + Duquesnoy
Graduate Engineers · Landscape Architects

→ 44

Köpenicker Strasse 187/188
D-10997 Berlin
T +49.30.6112218
F +49.30.6112686
info@thomanek-duquesnoy.de
www.thomanek-duquesnoy.de

TOPOTEK 1
Gesellschaft von Landschaftsarchitekten mbH

→ 194

Sophienstrasse 18
D-10178 Berlin
T +49.30.246258-0
F +49.30.246258-99
topotek1@topotek1.de
www.topotek1.de

Valentien + Valentien + Partners
Landscape Architects and Urban Planners

→ 116

Hauptstrasse 42
D-82234 Wessling
T +49.8153.952010
F +49.8153.952014
valentien@valentien.de
www.valentien.de

ver.de Landscape architecture
Birgit Kröniger · Jochen Rümpelein ·
Robert Wenk
→ 16

Ganzenmüllerstrasse 7
D-85354 Freising
T +49.8161.140993
F +49.8161.140996
info@gruppe-ver.de
www.gruppe-ver.de

Vogt Landscape Architects
Günther Vogt

→ 276, 324

Stampfenbachstrasse 57
CH-8006 Zurich
T +41.44.3605454
F +41.44.3605455
mail@vogt-la.ch
www.vogt-la.ch

Peter Walker and Partners
Landscape Architecture

→ 40, 316

739 Allston Way
USA–Berkeley, CA 94710
T +1.510.8499494
F +1 510.8499333
berkeley@pwpla.com
www.pwpla.com

Wartner & Zeitzler Landshut/Plattling
Helmut Wartner · Rupert Zeitzler

→ 264, 312

Bismarckplatz 18
D-84034 Landshut
T +49.871.23566
F +49.871.89006
wartner.zeitzler@t-online.de
www.wartner-zeitzler.de

wbp Landscape Architects Engineers
Christine Wolf · Rebekka Junge

→ 162

Nordring 49
D-44787 Bochum
T. +49.234.96299-0
F. +49.234.96299-25
mail@wbp-landschaftsarchitekten.de
www.wbp-landschaftsarchitekten.de

Werkgemeinschaft Freiraum
Gerd Aufmkolk · Franz Hirschmann ·
Rainer Sinke
→ 100

Vordere Cramergasse 11
D-90478 Nürnberg
T +49.911.94603-0
F +49.911.94603-10
info@wgf-nuernberg.de
www.wgf-nuernberg.de

WES & Partners · Landscape Architects
Hinnerk Wehberg · Peter Schatz ·
Wolfgang Betz · Michael Kaschke
→ 32, 48, 232

Jarrestrasse 80
D-22303 Hamburg
T +49.40.27841-0
F +49.40.2706668
info@wesup.de
www.wesup.de

Harms Wulf
Landscape Architects

→ 240

Oranienstrasse 183
D-10999 Berlin
T +49.30.6146883
F +49.30.6148515
la.wulf@t-online.de
www.harmswulf-landschaftsarchitekten.de

Object Index

Picture Credits

archiscape 7 a., 171–173 | asp 343 b. | Atelier LOIDL 187–189 | Aufmkolk, Gerd, Werkgemeinschaft Freiraum / Scheuerer, Manuela 101 m., 101 b., 102 | Becsei, Stephan 237–239 | Bobal, Martin 25 b. | Bode, Udo 29-31 | Boemans, Eva Maria 45–47 | Branzk, Maik 310 a. l., 310 b., 311 | Bühler, Achim 225 b. | BUGA 2005 185 a. | Burger, Horst 183, 184 a. r. | Burger, Susanne 66, 67 a. l. | Christoph Leib Photography Berlin 81–83 | cutting edge/Schulz, Jens 241–242 | Därr, Matthias 89–91 | Dempf, Christine 13–15 | Deutsche Steinkohle AG 159 b. | DIPOL Landscape Architects 141 b. | DMW – architekturbild Dominique Marc Wehrli, Christine Müller 289 b., 291 | Dolderer, Heinz 341, 342, 343 a. | Drecker, Peter 159 a., 160 a., 161 a. | Dreppenstedt, Claas 105–107, 87 b. l. | Emmenlauer, David 285–287 | Engel, Gerrit 65, 67 a. r. | Färber, Wolfgang 223 m., 224 a. r., 224 b. r., 337, 338 a., 339 | Fiorito, Massimo 321, 323 a. | Forster, Robin 137–139 | Gahl, Christian 233 a. | Gaudlitz, Frank 49 a., 50 a. l. | Giersch, Steffen/Rehwaldt Landscape Architects 175–177 | Girot, Christoph 73–75 | Gleinser Deak Communication Design Wolpertswede 133–135 | Golling, Brigitte 17 a. l., 18 a., 19 a. | Gräßle, Christoph 101 a., 103 a. | greenbox 160 b. | Green City Zurich/Hoch, G. 141 m., 142 a., 142 b. | Gruppe F 85 b., 85 a., 87 b. r. | GTL 179–181 | Günther, Wolfgang 223 a. | Gurr, Nicolaus 229–231 | Haberkern, Karin 208 m. | Hagen, Katrin/Meingaffner, Sophie 191–193 | Häfner/Jiménez 94 m., 94 b. | Heinkich, 121, 123 a. l., 123 b. | Hejduk, Pez 102 a. r. | Heumann, Michael 223 b., 225 a. | Hinze, Thorsten 333–335 | Holzherr, Florian 125, 127 | hutterreimann + cejka 301, 302 a. l., 303 | Jaipmann 309, 310 a. r. | Jakob AG, Trubschachen 141 a., 142 m. | Janot, Christoph 163 a. | Joosten, Hans 7 b., 195–197, 199–201 | Jühling und Bertram Landscape Architects 113–115 | Kluska, Peter 9 a., 61–63, 261–263 | Krafft-Wehberg 234/235 | Lafarge Zement/Halama 254/255 | Landscape Architecture and Ecology, Angela Bezzenberger 57–59 | Latitude Nord – Gilles Vexlard + Laurence Vacherot 185 b. | Latz, Michael 117, 119, 167 b., 167 m., 168 a. r. | Latz + Partners 168 a. l. | Leidorf, Klaus 265 a. | Leppert, Stefan 155–157 | Libuda, Christo/Poreski, Franziska 203–205 | lohrer.hochrein landscape architects 123 a. r. | Loidl-Reisch, Cordula 21, 22 | Lucks, Stefan Wolf 305–307 | Lüttge, Thomas 129–131 | Mai 93 b., 93 m. | Meingaffner, Sophie/Hagen, Katrin 191–193 | MRG/Rüdiger Haase 184 a. l. | Müller, Diana 224 a. l., 338 b. | Müller, Frank-Heinrich 207 | Müller, Harald F. 257 a. | Müller, Jean 249 m., 250 a. l. | Müller-Naumann, Stefan, Munich 9 b. | Muhs, Andreas 85 m., 86, 87 a. | Myrzik/Jarisch 273–275 | nan 151 | Niemeyer, Wolfgang Hermann 269, 270 a. r., 271 | Office for Urban Development and Environment, Hamburg 330 | Panick 167 a. | Peter Walker and Partners 317–319, 41–43 | Poreski, Franziska/Libuda, Christo 203–205 | Porsche/GFA Leipzig 94 a. | realgrün Landscape Architects 109, 110 | Rego, Marta/bauchplan 25 a., 26/27 | Rehwaldt Landscape Architects/Giersch, Steffen 175–177 | relais landscape architects 219–221 | Ritz, Wolfgang 322, 323 b. | RMP Landscape Architects 215–217 | Rockinger, Andreas 297, 298 | Rotzler Krebs Partners 145 a., 146 a. l., 147 a. r., 289 a., 290, 294 a. r. | Schambeck Schmitt GbR 210 a. l. | Scheffel, Claudia 208 b. | Scheuerer, Manuela/Aufmkolk, Gerd, Werkgemeinschaft Freiraum 101 b., 101 m., 102 | Schmidt, Rainer/Mittzow, Michael 253 | Schmidt, Rainer/Müller-Naumann, Stefan 281–283 | Schmidt, Rainer/Sistoli Schnell, Raffaella 69–71 | Scholz, Hendrik 257 b., 258, 259 | Schulz, Jens/cutting edge 241, 242 | Schulz, Jens/van den Ende, Aeliana 77–79 | Schwager, Christian 145 b., 146 a. r., 147 a. l., 147 b. | Seelemann, Dirk 208 a., 209 a. | Stock, Wolfram 250 a. r., 250 b., 251 r. | Stötzer Neher Landscape Architects 245–247 | Stoldt, Henning/Bendfeldt Schröder Franke 37–39, 329–331 | Strauß, Dietmar 97, 99, 53–55 | Thiel, Reiner 211–213 | Tollerian, Dietmar 149, 150 | Valentien 184 b. | van den Ende, Aeliana/Schulz, Jens 77–79 | ver.de landscape architecture 17 b. l., 17 a. r., 19 b. | Vogt, Christian 277, 279, 327 | Vogt Landscape Architects/Waldmeister, Jürg 325, 326 | Wicky, Gaston 293, 294 a. l., 495 a. | Walter/GFA Leipzig 93 a. | Wartner & Zeitzler 313–315, 265 b., 266/267 | wbp Landscape Architects and Engineers 163 b., 164/165 | Wels, Peter 35 | WES & Partners 49 b., 50 b., 33 b., 34 | Wolf, Thomas 249 a., 249 b., 251 r.

Cover
front side picture: Dietmar Strauß | front side plan: Wolfgang Färber | back side right: DMW – architekturbild Dominique Marc Wehrli, Christine Müller | back side left: Marta Rego/bauchplan